MEDIATION
AND
ARBITRATION

Cavendish
Publishing
Limited

MEDIATION AND ARBITRATION

Dr Peter d'Ambrumenil
MBBS (Lond), MRCS (Eng), LRCP (Lond), ACIArb

First published in Great Britain 1997 by Cavendish Publishing Limited, The Glass House, Wharton Street, London WC1X 9PX.
Telephone: 0171-278 8000 Facsimile: 0171-278 8080

d'Ambrumenil, Peter Lance
Mediation and arbitration
1. Arbitration and award – England 2. Dispute resolution – (Law) – England 3. Mediation – Law and legislation – England
I. Title
344.2'079

1-85941-155-X

Printed and bound in Great Britain

FOREWORD

Those who have shown an interest in the 'medico-legal practitioner's series' may like to learn something about its origins and the history of its development. With this objective in mind I will devote a few moments to the past and I will then turn to the future which is, after all, even more important for us.

I first conceived the idea of such a theme in the Summer of 1994. By that stage I had been preparing reports for lawyers on cases of alleged medical negligence for about five years. I had also been looking at other doctors' reports for the same length of time and it was becoming increasingly apparent to me that one of the lawyers' most difficult tasks was to understand the medical principles clearly. To be fair to the lawyers, there were some doctors who did not always make matters very clear. This, coupled with the difficulty which many doctors have in understanding the legal concept of negligence and related topics, merely served to compound the problem.

It therefore occurred to me that a possible solution to the difficulty would be to develop some material on medical topics written by doctors who had a particular interest in the medico-legal field. The authors would require at least four attributes. First, they would have to be specialists in their own field. Secondly, they would need the ability to explain their subject to non-medical readers in clear language that was easy to follow. Put another way there was no case for writing a medical textbook for their students or colleagues. Thirdly, they would require a fair amount of experience in medico-legal reporting, analysis of cases and dealing with lawyers who were defending or advancing cases. This would give them an understanding of how the lawyer's mind works and an appreciation of the medical areas which can cause difficulty in practice and where accidents can happen. There would be a contrast with medical books where the emphasis is on the diseases which most commonly present to the doctor. Fourthly, the authors would need the ability to work in harmony with a series editor who was anxious to achieve some degree of uniformity across the whole range of the material.

Having identified these four points as being desirable characteristics of the potential authors the next step was to find a publisher who would be sufficiently interested to give the project the support it needed. This was to be no small task and was likely to involve a very long term commitment because, after the initial launch, it was inevitable that much more work would be required by way of future editions and additional titles. I was most fortunate to be dealing with Cavendish Publishing in connection with my own book, *The General Practitioner and the Law of Negligence,* and I am pleased to say that they seized this new idea with the utmost enthusiasm. At last I thought that the 'medico-legal practitioner series' would become a reality.

It then only remained to find the authors, commission the work and wait for the results. It was at this point, however, that I began to realise that I was still only at the very beginning of my task. Eventually, however, after numerous discussions with various people a team materialised. When the early chapters of the first books began to arrive it was starting to look as though we really were going to have something which was quite unique. When the final manuscripts arrived my confidence increased still further. More than two years after my initial plans the first set of books has become available and the dream has turned into reality.

This, then, is how the project came into being but it must be emphasised that, in a manner of speaking, we have really only just got ourselves started. For the series to thrive it must be flexible and respond to the needs of its users. It must adapt to medical developments and legal changes. Clinical subjects are a primary consideration but it is my firm intention to expand the series to involve other areas of interest. Indeed the first non-clinical title should appear almost as soon as the initial set becomes available. On a more long term basis, I would like the series to cover every field of expertise that is of concern to the medico-legal practitioner.

Uniformity of approach and clarity of presentation must be hallmarks of the individual titles but the series as a whole must be independent and objective. If we can aspire to these criteria we should achieve a fair measure of success in assisting our readers to give good advice to their clients.

It remains for me to express my gratitude to all the authors and to the publishers for their cooperation. In another kind of way I will be equally grateful to all our readers for placing their reliance on us and for sharing our optimism.

Walter Scott

Series Editor

Slough

August 1996

* * *

Dr Peter d'Ambrumenil's practical book *Mediation and Arbitration* is both very good and very timely.

Everyone involved in pursuing and defending compensation claims faces increasing pressure to find a speedy and cost-effective way of obtaining a fair result.

Increasingly specialised skills and techniques used on both sides produce greater cost for both pursuing and defending claims. Great changes are likely as a result of the reduced availability of Legal Aid and proposals to reduce Legal Aid lawyers' remuneration, through the progressive replacement of Legal Aid with 'no win: no fee' conditional fee agreements, and from the final report of the Woolf Committee 'Access to Justice' reinforcing the pressure for Alternative Disputes Resolution.

The overview in this book of the options available for resolving disputes by some form of mediation and arbitration, short of pursuing full scale civil court proceedings to trial will be valuable to most claimants, claims lawyers, insurers, and institutions faced with claims, who have not previously been required to consider Alternative Dispute Resolution seriously.

The worked out examples of actual cases discussed in this book bring the discussion to life. Some of the original initiatives used to resolve the decided cases reveal the wide range of practical remedies that can be applied through mediation which are not available to a trial judge.

This book is much needed at this point in time.

Peter Latham
October 1996

New Court Chambers
5 Verulam Buildings
Gray's Inn
London WC1R 5LY

ACKNOWLEDGMENTS

The Author wishes to express his thanks to the following Persons and Organisations:

The United Nations Commission on International Trade Law for permission to reproduce The UNCITRAL Arbitration Rules and The UNCITRAL Model Law on International Commercial Arbitration.

Her Majesty's Stationery Office for permission to reproduce extracts from the Arbitration Act 1996 and the various High Court Forms, all of which are Crown or Parliamentary copyright.

To the many friends and colleagues who helped by reading the drafts and making the many helpful and productive comments, and in particular my thanks are due to:

Marilyn Francis, my secretary for patiently reading and correcting drafts of this book

Peter Dobie for his many helpful comments

David Grimley for much valuable advice and comment

Peter Buechel for reading and commenting upon the draft text

Neil Tweed for careful attention to the text and content

The American Trial Lawyers Association who generously provided material for this book as did the Australian Commercial Disputes Centre

Brian Robertson for his generous and helpful comments

This book is dedicated to my wife Sarah without whose forbearance, support and encouragement, I could never have written it.

CONTENTS

Contents

CHAPTER ONE

INTRODUCTORY REMARKS

This chapter comprises a short history of litigation in its various forms. It is a brief but informative source of information and it is hoped that it will assist the reader to understand both the principles of the procedures outlined later in this book and provide an idea as to why some of these procedures have arisen.

Litigation is as old as man himself. Since the day he came down from his tree or, if you prefer, climbed out of the ocean, several facts have been certain. It has always been certain that having been born he would die; it has also been said that the inevitability of taxes is another fact. One fact, however, which is as certain as death is that as long as man exists he will disagree with another man and will have to be 'sorted out by a third man', and so came about litigation.

BIBLICAL JUSTICE

In biblical times disputes were common and the means of resolving them legion; one only has to remember the episode of the wisdom of Solomon who, threatening to slice a child in half, caused an immediate resolution of the dispute and an equitable solution resulted.

THE NEED FOR ALTERNATIVE METHODS OF RESOLVING DISPUTES

As time went on it became apparent to those who were in commerce and, to a lesser extent, to those who governed them that if the country and its economy were to survive an alternative method of resolving these disputes was going to be essential, and hopefully it would be a method which would allow those in dispute to continue trading, because such is the nature of commerce.

THE ROMANS

The ideal method has yet to be found, but in Roman times the Merchants, who in many cases were not able to use the courts, which were only accessible to Roman citizens, set up a system whereby others could resolve conflicts. The method was one in which the parties to a dispute would consult a wise man (the Praetor) from their community, whose knowledge of the affairs was deemed to be greater than most and whose sense of justice was respected by those involved.

He was then invited to consider the evidence and give a decision which those in dispute agreed to accept as binding upon them. Thus was born arbitration.

PROGRESS IN ENGLAND

As time went on and England returned to the dark ages, trial by combat appeared and was not finally dispatched from the statute books until 1816, although its use had by then, thankfully, fallen into disrepute.

Trial by combat

In 1816 a case of libel resulted in the plaintiff claiming his right to trial by combat. The defendant, a man of lesser stature, chose not to defend the matter. Shortly after this Parliament abolished it.

The system of trial by combat certainly encouraged the parties to a dispute to consider other methods of litigating than through the courts and it may well be that the Lord Chancellors of the time had a similar motive to the present one. The result of all this was that, again, arbitration began to be used, albeit informally and outside the state system.

Napoleonic and English common law

As civilisation progressed the English common law system evolved, and on the continent the system based upon the Napoleonic code began to develop. Both became sophisticated systems but both differed in their approach to the legal problems.

Nevertheless the citizens of the lands all had the same basic commercial requirement, which was for a simple system by which disputes could be resolved.

On the continent, a system which was primarily inquisitorial began to develop, whilst in England the predominantly adversarial system was to gain a hold.

The English court system

Over the last year the tendency of the courts has been to actively encourage Alternative Dispute Resolution and Lord Woolf through his active encouragement of parties to move away from adversarial means of resolving disputes has done much to persuade parties to litigation that the concurrent use of mediation is of great importance. He has more recently instigated other more appropriate forms of encouragement such as 'fast track litigation' with the attendant reduction in costs and fixed price litigation which must of necessity persuade those advising parties that early settlement is to the advantage of the litigant and his lawyer.

More will be said of this later in the book.

ARBITRATION

In all cases the governments felt a need to control and yet to encourage these 'alternative courts'. The need to do so arose from a twofold purpose. First there was a need to ensure that the systems were supervised by the courts, as no civilisation can justify its courts being ousted, and yet this needs to be tempered because if the system is to work it must be credible, and this means that decisions reached through the system must be enforceable.

This has brought about a relative mass of legislation and regulation all of which purport to do just what is outlined in the above paragraph.

Cost of courts encourages arbitration

This having been said, the tendency in England is for Alternative Dispute Resolution to become both desirable and effective. One of the main reasons for this is the desire of government to reduce the use made of the civil courts by means of punitive increase in the fees charged to those who attempt to access the system. When these charges are added to the costs of representation and the reduction in eligibility for Legal Aid, the result is a need for an alternative system by which those in dispute can have the matter resolved.

It is accepted that the parties have to pay for arbitration proceedings, but the cost of litigation should not be forgotten. If the dispute is resolved on the basis of documents only, the cost is infinitesimal when compared with the full panoply of litigation.

When considering an arbitration which proceeds to a full hearing the parties will in both cases have to pay for the legal advice and representation, but in the case of the arbitration they additionally have to pay for the arbitrator. However, a good arbitrator will probably act more like an official referee than a judge with the effect that the proceedings are expedited and many matters resolved before the matter comes to trial.

MEDIATION AND EQUITY

One of the prime benefits of mediation is that not only can goodwill or good trading relationships be kept between the parties, but it is possible also to obtain an equitable resolution, which can be translated into common parlance as a resolution which the parties consider to be fair and reasonable.

MEDICAL ISSUES AND ADR

This book is predominantly aimed at those involved in medical litigation, and here several other factors are involved. One of the most important is a need for the plaintiff to have some degree of protection against the inevitable publicity which will follow the public mention of matters which would otherwise be deemed to be too sensitive to mention outside the doctor-patient relationship. Another is the need for a doctor, usually the defendant, to avoid unnecessary damage to his professional reputation.

Both these factors assist the parties in their decision to go to an alternative method of resolving their dispute. The term ADR encompasses a number of processes which are either alternatives to litigation or which will help resolve issues which have already reached litigation or arbitration.

Discipline and standards

Inevitably the counter argument arises that patients need to have the doctor dealt with publicly in order to ensure standards are kept high and professional retribution is visited upon the man whose standard of practice deserves it.

This argument can be dealt with swiftly since the various professional bodies are always available to deal with such disciplinary matters, and the results of a court action are not of significant consequence to any disciplinary tribunal considering the case.

The other side of this argument is that if the matter is not dealt with through the courts, patients will launch and pursue needless cases against the profession. This argument is groundless and there is no evidence of any consequence available to support it.

The benefit to the parties

The benefits to both parties cannot be overestimated and the only significant hurdle which is in the way of more cases being dealt with through alternative methods of dispute resolution is the fact that, at the present time, there is no means of public funding for those wishing to progress their claim through arbitration or indeed through any of the other methods of dispute resolution.

Legal Aid

If these methods are to be encouraged by the government, there will need to be a system whereby the proceedings can be financed without prejudicing the position of those who would otherwise be in receipt of Legal Aid. The proposals put forward by Lord Woolf contain much in respect of costs and funding to persuade the reluctant party to view mediation favourably.

The insurers' approach

It is notable that some insurers are taking the view that they will indemnify the other party against such charges and where they are legally aided this is not so unreasonable since even if the defendant wins his case, he will not obtain an order for costs against the legally aided plaintiff. He thus has a reason to keep his own costs down even where his case is unassailable.

Mediation

Mediation will be fully explained later but in essence it is a procedure by which an independent third party attempts to help those in dispute to bring about a resolution of that dispute.

Encouragement from the courts

The courts have now recognised Alternative Dispute Resolution and in a number of well publicised Practice Directions, the legal advisers to litigants have been for the first time obliged to consider the applicability of mediation and advise the court whether its use has been considered. There was, however, little beyond this to encourage the parties to use it and certainly until there is a penalty in costs it is improbable that mediation will be a serious contender for most medical litigation.

CONCILIATION

Conciliation is a term frequently interchanged with mediation. Within this book however it is taken only to refer to the procedure incorporated in NHS complaints procedures and not procedures used in resolution of commercial disputes where it is held to be utterly respectable. It is touched on in this chapter if only to say that it has no place in cases where litigation is contemplated by the parties.

CHAPTER TWO

ARBITRATION – AN INTRODUCTION

Arbitration is the term used to describe a number of procedures which can aptly be classed as providing a means of dispute resolution with a certain outcome.

INTRODUCTORY REMARKS

There are a number of essential prerequisites to an arbitration and amongst these is the necessity for the parties to agree to submit themselves to the process.

Once it has been decided that a dispute has arisen, the parties will need to consider how they are to respond to it.

Traditionally, the immediate response has been to instruct a lawyer, where applicable 'sign the Legal Aid Forms' and then sit back intermittently confirming the lawyer's instructions, as dictated by the lawyer.

The defendant, on the other hand, may receive his first notion of a problem in the Letter Before Action, upon receipt of which he reaches for his 'insurance policy' advises his insurers, and then sits back consuming increased volumes of drink to placate his injured pride and nerves.

ENTRY TO ARBITRATION

If arbitration is the decided method of dispute resolution, most of the above will still be necessary and there is no means of avoiding the necessity for sound legal management.

The advantages

Why then arbitrate? Arbitration has the advantage of being a definitive means of resolving a dispute with a certain outcome. This latter word denotes a final and enforceable settlement, enforcement being possible through the courts of the land.

The advantage of arbitration is that the parties can appoint their own specified arbitrator, who will consider the evidence and decide the outcome. This means that it is possible to appoint someone who is knowledgeable of the subject-matter of the dispute, thus relieving the parties of the necessity and expense to adduce as much expert evidence.

The arbitrator is not allowed to 'give himself' evidence but he can and should use his expert knowledge to interpret the evidence provided by the parties.

It is of the greatest importance that an arbitration can be almost as formal or informal as the parties require. It is necessary that certain formalities are kept and complied with if the award is to be enforceable.

This means that the arbitration can be kept within very simple lines and with very little formality, provided that the rules of natural justice are complied with and provided the relatively simple requirements of the Arbitration Act are complied with.

Later in this book there is a chapter on arbitration which discusses in some detail the most comprehensive procedural requirements. These, however, are phrased in such a way that they reflect the most formal end of arbitration which is in a number of ways akin to court procedures and therefore more expensive than the simpler procedures which although not so formal provide an equal degree of equity and justice.

The simpler the process the cheaper it will be and it should be recalled that there is no obligation upon parties to have advocates or if they decide upon advocates there is no reason that they should appoint legally qualified persons.

Having said this it must be remembered that an arbitration can and usually should be a simple procedure resulting in a just and proper outcome. The parties can decide upon a minimal of pleadings resulting in a simple exchange of documents as outlined under 'Documents Only Arbitrations'. This can be accompanied by an attendance at a hearing, at which the statements can be expanded upon. A limited number of witnesses can be agreed and if all the expert witnesses can produce agreed reports their attendance becomes superfluous.

With careful attention to the issues, identification of those issues which are actually disputed and, with fine attention to the types of witnesses, the case can be settled by the arbitrator for a much lower fee than if all issues remain disputed and every possible witness is called.

The arbitrator can do much to help the parties reach the situation where the case can be simply dealt with.

SHOULD I GO TO ARBITRATION?

Whether or not the parties could and should enter into an arbitration will depend upon a number of factors.

If there is an agreement between the parties to refer any dispute between themselves to arbitration, this will bind them to do so and will probably describe the manner in which the arbitrator should be appointed. An example of such a specified method of appointment would be the typical clause in a partnership agreement dealing with the manner in which partnership disputes should be managed.

More usually, in these circumstances, it will be a decision made between the parties, after the dispute has arisen, which will result in the matter being referred to an arbitrator. It will, in these circumstances, be necessary for the parties to agree to forgo their right to litigation in preference to submitting the dispute to arbitration.

COMPOSITION OF THE TRIBUNAL

Having so agreed, the next decision to be made is to decide upon the make up of the tribunal; the phrase given to describe the person or persons appointed to act as arbitrators.

Deciding upon an arbitrator requires that the parties take some care, and another way to avoid any further acrimony is to request a third party to make the choice and appoint a suitable candidate.

In most cases a single arbitrator will suffice and indeed if carefully chosen will avoid the later need for much of the procedure and evidence which would be essential if the matter was to be put before a judge in the courts.

Hopefully the parties will feel able to agree upon an appointment of a single arbitrator. If this is not possible each may nominate a single arbitrator, giving rise to a tribunal of two. It is prudent to have a tribunal which is comprised of odd numbers of people as this avoids the situation of a 'tie' and the resulting difficulty in coming to a proper decision.

The candidate should be able to understand both the technical medical issues and should also have sufficient understanding of the law and procedure to make a proper judicial decision. (More will be said of this in a later part of this book.)

If it is decided that the parties are content with a tribunal of two, the tribunal should of its own volition appoint a third person as an umpire. In the event that the tribunal cannot reach a decision then the umpire takes over and makes the decision which is binding on the parties as if made by the original tribunal.

Failing this, they may ask an independent body to make an appointment which is binding upon them.

HOW TO PROCEED WITH THE APPOINTMENT OF AN ARBITRATOR

Having decided who should be invited to act as arbitrator, an approach should be made to the proposed candidate to enquire as to whether they would be prepared to act.

Section 5 of the Arbitration Act 1996 provides that if the agreement to the arbitration is in writing the provisions of the Act shall be deemed to apply to the arbitration.

The implications of appointing an arbitrator

It must be understood that the arbitration process is a 'private agreement' by the parties to submit their dispute to resolution by a third party.

The law takes the view that such agreement needs to be supported and it will be seen from other sections of the Act that the level of support provided from both the Act and the ability of the courts to support and strengthen the inherent powers of the arbitrator are much more than is generally reckoned. In general terms it can be stated that the courts will not, without good reason, interfere with either the conduct of the proceedings or the award, and they will support the arbitrator if and when required by providing additional powers should they be required.

Appointment in writing or otherwise

Under s 5 the appointment needs to be in writing but under s 2(a) it is not necessary for the agreement to be signed and under s 6 it is stated that reference to anything being written includes its being recorded by any means.

The formality of the appointment

A suitable form of appointment would be the following:

Whereas a dispute has arisen between us, we agree to refer the matters in dispute, which appear in the schedule to this agreement, to AB, whom we appoint as Arbitrator, with authority to decide the issues and make an Award, under the terms of the Arbitration Act 1996. Dated the   day of

Signed ....

Signed ....

Acceptance of appointment by arbitrator

Assuming that he is willing to be appointed, he should be asked to confirm his appointment in writing, and confirm that there is no reason known to him why he should not act. He may at the same time advise the parties of his intentions in respect of the procedure to be adopted.

Agreement to submit future dispute to arbitration

It is possible in a contractual relationship to agree to submit any future dispute to arbitration. This situation is, however, unlikely to arise in medical disputes.

In the case of medical disputes where the claimant is an injured third party as in personal injury claims for injuries sustained in an accident, it is likely that there is not a contractual relationship with the insurer or the other party.

In cases of medical negligence it is again improbable that there will be any such contractual duty to submit a dispute to arbitration. In the National Health Service the patient has no contractual relationship with the doctor and in private practice it is, in England, exceedingly uncommon to have a written contract incorporating such a term between the parties.

Dispute over appointment of arbitrators

One circumstance which is not very likely to arise in the field of medical disputes is the appointment of an arbitrator in circumstances where difficulties have arisen and the law or the courts have to support the other party.

Firstly, where it is agreed that the parties will each appoint an arbitrator, but only one does, s 17(1) of the Arbitration Act 1996 provides that the party having duly appointed his arbitrator, may give notice to the other that in default he proposes to appoint his nominee to act as sole arbitrator.

Where the circumstances of the case are such that there is no specific agreement between the parties as to how the arbitrator(s) should be appointed the party or parties may apply to the courts who will make an appropriate appointment under s 18.

THE IMMUNITY OF THE ARBITRATOR

One very recent change in the law concerns the immunity of the arbitrator and appointing authorities. Until the passing of the Arbitration Act 1996 the position of an arbitrator in relation to litigation was, to say the least, uncertain. It was almost certainly correct to say that if he was negligent as opposed to acting in bad faith, any party who sustained a loss as a result of the action or omission had it open to them to sue. This was a very unfortunate position and did nothing to protect the arbitrator from the threat of coercion arising from this pressure. Whilst there is no recorded evidence that this ever had an effect upon an arbitrator's independence, the law has now been changed to confirm what was previously the practical position. Section 29 of the Arbitration Act 1996 reads as follows:

> **29** – (1) An arbitrator is not liable for anything done or omitted in the discharge or purported discharge of his functions as an arbitrator unless the act or omission is shown to have been in bad faith.
>
> (2) Subsection (1) applies to an employee or agent of an arbitrator as it applies to the arbitrator himself.
>
> (3) This section does not affect any liability incurred by an arbitrator by reason of his resigning (but see section 25 of the Arbitration Act 1996, which refers to the resignation of the arbitrator).

Immunity of appointing bodies

Section 74 of the Arbitration Act 1996 extends this immunity to persons or institutions requested to nominate an arbitrator.

REMOVAL OF ARBITRATOR

Before considering the actual terms of the agreement it is worth looking at the security of the arbitrator. Considering his position in what can safely be described as a 'private judge', it is important that he cannot be removed from his position by anyone for reasons of less than meritorious motive. Section 23 of the Arbitration Act 1996 provides that the parties acting jointly may revoke the authority of the arbitrator, the safeguard that the revocation must be in writing is incorporated in s 23(4).

The courts are also, in s 24, vested with the power to remove an arbitrator, the specific circumstances being clearly laid out.

With these two sections being read together the security of the arbitrator is sound and he cannot be removed for other than good reason.

THE POWER OF THE ARBITRATOR

Having considered the appointment of the arbitrator it is necessary to consider the terms of the agreement. Broadly speaking, the parties to the Arbitration Agreement have almost complete authority to decide upon the way in which the arbitration should take place and the powers to provide the arbitrator with.

COMPARISON OF ARBITRATION ACT AND PARTNERSHIP ACT

The Arbitration Act is, in many ways, similar to the Partnership Act of 1890 in that it provides a basic set of rules by which an arbitration should be conducted to which the parties can, to a great extent, add to or exclude by mutual agreement.

Procedural rules

In the majority of arbitrations, whether they be on the basis of consideration of documents only or on oral evidence, the arbitrator will be appointed and will decide upon the 'rules under which the proceedings will be conducted'.

There are a number of schemes in existence under which the arbitral procedure can be conducted and these include schemes for consumers run under the auspices of the Chartered Institute of Arbitrators. Similar schemes are run by various organisations within the building industry and then there are a number of sets of rules such as UNCITRAL Arbitration Rules, a very comprehensive set of rules designed for use in both the domestic and international field.

The present Arbitration Act 1996 draws very heavily on the UNCITRAL model law but by no means enacts the entire draft.

The Arbitration Act and medical claims

For the purposes of the type of arbitration envisaged in the field of medical negligence or personal injury, the present Arbitration Act with its default powers provides a very adequate framework for the arbitration process.

This could be a reasonable place to consider some of the possibilities which the arbitrator could adopt, although later in this book the various procedures will be discussed in greater detail.

DOCUMENTS ONLY ARBITRATIONS

If the dispute is a relatively small one, say under £10,000, it might be appropriate to have the arbitrator consider submissions made in writing. The arbitrator would normally invite the claimant (party making the claim), to send his written submissions within a period of say 14 days. Any submissions should simultaneously be served upon the respondent (person against whom the claim is being made).

Within 14 days of service of the submissions prepared by the claimant, the respondent should serve his own submissions. It would be usual for the arbitrator to allow a further 14 days for any replies that the claimant wishes to submit and then the arbitrator would consider the evidence and prepare his award (judgment).

Even if it has been agreed that the dispute should be settled on the basis of written submissions the Arbitration Act allow either party or the arbitrator to ask for a hearing. (Procedure and implications of the hearing will be discussed later in much greater detail.)

FULL HEARING ARBITRATIONS

If it has been decided that the matter should be resolved by a 'full arbitration', the arbitrator will, after his appointment, probably invite the parties to a preliminary meeting at which procedure will be discussed in great detail.

ARBITRATOR'S REMUNERATION

It is imperative that prior to accepting his appointment as an arbitrator, the terms of engagement including the level of remuneration should be agreed as once the contract is 'struck' it is no longer possible for the arbitrator to insist upon terms being inserted into the contract and if remuneration is not conclusively agreed upon he may be thrown upon the tender mercies of a court taxing Master. This has significant potential for causing grief, the Taxing Master being an official of the court charged with deciding upon the level of payment which should be made when the law or the parties' contract requires such an officer to make the decisions. Those who have had fees subject to such a process will realise the importance of avoiding contact with this process.

CHAPTER THREE

ARBITRATION – PRELIMINARY PROBLEMS

Some problems associated with arbitrations are not understood and provide traps for the unwary.

CHALLENGE TO THE ARBITRATOR'S JURISDICTION

A not uncommon preliminary problem that the arbitrator faces is a challenge to his jurisdiction. The reasons may be legion but the likelihood is a frustrated party making every effort to delay or derail the proceedings.

Until the advent of the Arbitration Act 1996, it was considered that an arbitrator could not decide his own jurisdiction. In *Harbour Assurance Co (UK) Ltd v Kansa General International Insurance Co Ltd* (1993), it was held that there was no reason why an arbitrator should not rule upon whether the arbitration clause was void for illegality.

The Arbitration Act 1996 under s 30 clarifies the arbitrator's position and states under s 30(1):

30 – (1) Unless otherwise agreed by the parties, the Arbitral Tribunal may rule on its own substantive jurisdiction that is, as to –

(a) whether there is a valid arbitration agreement;

(b) whether the tribunal is properly constituted; and

(c) what matters have been submitted to arbitration in accordance with the arbitration agreement.

A right of appeal is provided by s 2, as follows:

(2) Any such ruling may be challenged by any available arbitral process of appeal or review or in accordance with the provisions of this Part.

DEALING WITH A CHALLENGE TO JURISDICTION

In practice if a challenge is made the arbitrator should hear the representations of the parties, following which he should decide whether there is any doubt as to his jurisdiction. If he concludes that there is any doubt he has two major routes open to him. The first is to accept the jurisdiction and proceed with the arbitration. If he does this he should obtain undertakings from the appropriate party that in the event that the award is later held to be void his fees will be met.

The second, and possibly more prudent, course of action is for him to refuse to proceed and invite the parties to obtain a decision from the court. The resulting application to the courts will result in a declaration or an injunction, depending upon whether his jurisdiction is accepted.

If the arbitrator has decided erroneously that he has the jurisdiction and has made an award, then the decision of the court will, if it decides he did not have such jurisdiction, be an order setting aside the award.

CHAPTER FOUR

ARBITRATION – THE PRELIMINARY MEETING

There are many issues which can and should be dealt with at the preliminary meeting.

INTRODUCTORY ISSUES

An arbitration agreement gives rise to an arbitrator or arbitrators, who are referred to as the 'tribunal'.

Assuming that there is no challenge to the arbitrator's jurisdiction or that he has ruled that he has the jurisdiction, he may proceed with the preliminary meeting.

Attention will be given to as many of the procedures as are expedient and these will include checking that the arbitration agreement is valid and determining who is to be referred to as the claimant and who is to be referred to as the respondent. In practice this usually presents little problem as the person initiating the claim will be the claimant.

The arbitrator will note whether the parties are to be represented, and if so, by whom, and indeed whether counsel is to be instructed or whether the parties will represent themselves or use technically competent advocates.

The meeting provides an opportunity to identify the matters in dispute.

EXCLUSION AGREEMENTS

Any exclusion agreements need to be considered.

Exclusion agreements are agreements to exclude the power of the courts to intervene in certain aspects of the proceedings. There is a basic assumption that the courts have an inherent power to supervise all inferior tribunals, but in certain, very specific, circumstances the parties may voluntarily exclude this right.

This right of the courts to supervise and generally interfere where appropriate is a right jealously protected by the courts. However, Parliament has considered this issue and decided that commercial expedience and thus the country's economy require that there should be certainty in the arbitral process. Thus in ss 45 and 69 of the Arbitration Act 1996 it enacted a restricted right for the parties to exclude the jurisdiction of the courts in respect of a preliminary point of law or by s 69 the right of appeal to challenge the award (judgment of the arbitrator) on a point of law. Section 87 of the Arbitration Act provides that an agreement under ss 45 and 69 shall be void unless entered into after the commencement of the proceedings. This rule applies only to domestic arbitrations but as nearly all medical disputes will arise within this country, that is England and Wales; Scotland, Northern Ireland and the Channel Islands all being considered to be different jurisdictions. Thus, unless otherwise specified, all references are to arbitrations in England and Wales. It is probable that most medical disputes will arise within this jurisdiction.

A NOTE ON OTHER JURISDICTIONS

There are many other jurisdictions in the world each with their own legislation. Most of those who have systems based upon the English common law system have Arbitration Acts which in many ways mirror those of the Arbitration Act 1950.

Within the United Kingdom's province, the Channel Islands all have similar legislation as do Scotland and Northern Ireland.

PLEADINGS

The next matter which the arbitrator should consider and obtain agreement to (failing such agreement he should make an appropriate order), is the matter of pleadings. Pleadings are the basis of a well managed arbitration and are the series of documents prepared by each side stating succinctly their case. It must be remembered that pleadings should contain a statement of the facts upon which the party relies but should not state the evidence which it will adduce to support it.

The importance of well-drafted pleadings cannot be overestimated and the arbitrator has a duty to ensure that the parties fully appreciate the significance of the pleadings and that a bland denial to every paragraph of the statement of claim is unhelpful.

Well-drafted pleadings can, of their own accord, by helping the parties understand the claim, result in an early settlement, with an associated massive saving in costs.

It is not easy to state that one pleading is more important than the rest but the statement of claim which is the first of the pleadings has the potential, if well-drafted, to make for ease of comprehension of the case by the respondent. This in turn allows the defence to be succinct and applicable.

It thus behoves the parties, or other representatives acting on their behalf, to instruct their legal advisors to give full attention to this early and important aspect of the case.

Terminology

In the following text the traditional terms used in court proceedings will be used, but it should be noted that pleadings in an arbitration are commonly referred to as points of claim, points of defence, etc. The plaintiff is referred to as the claimant and the defendant is known as the respondent. These terms are used interchangeably throughout this text.

Preliminary orders

An order made by the arbitrator is an order which the parties must obey. He can enforce it by means of an adverse order in costs, or if there is a flagrant refusal by a party to comply either the arbitrator or a party may apply to the court to vest the arbitrator with the powers of a judge.

The arbitrator will at the preliminary meeting, if held, or in any event, order a timescale for the pleadings.

Such an order may be a consent order, which means that the parties have between themselves agreed to the terms of the order and the arbitrator is merely formalising it, but in this event it should be noted that the arbitrator cannot, without the further consent of the parties, amend it. Many arbitrators will therefore merely issue an order rather than a consent order.

The sequence of pleadings

Following upon the statement of claim and defence, the parties will often want further clarification of certain matters and thus will issue requests for further and better particulars. The response to these is provided by replies to requests for further and better particulars.

In some cases there is a counterclaim and where this is the case the party, upon being served with the statement of claim, will file a defence along with a counterclaim.

The original claimant will then have to reply to the counterclaim with his own defence.

DISCOVERY

Once the pleadings have closed, the parties will usually seek orders for discovery. Discovery is the process whereby either party attempts to find out what relevant documentation is held by the other party. In principle, all documents which are relevant to the case are discoverable, although some will be privileged. Documents which are discoverable are open to inspection by the opposing party.

The procedure for discovery is not dealt with in great detail as details can be sought in any standard text on procedure. However, it may be stated that the arbitrator will make an order for discovery incorporating an order that the parties shall exchange lists of documents within a given number of days after the close of pleadings.

The arbitrator will also order that a bundle of documents will be provided to him within a given number of days prior to the hearing.

WITNESSES

Witnesses fall into two major groups: witnesses of fact and expert witnesses.

At the preliminary meeting, the arbitrator will need to consider both types of witness. He will need to determine whether the parties will be calling expert evidence and if so how many experts it is anticipated will be necessary. As a general rule it can be anticipated that the parties will try to match each of the witnesses called by the other party.

Witness and statements

Whilst the arbitrator should be reasonable in acquiescing to the wishes of the parties in respect of types and numbers of expert witnesses to be called, he should also attempt to curb the wilder excesses of the over enthusiastic party.

Having determined what is reasonable he should make an order accordingly. The order should also provide for the experts to meet on a without prejudice basis (see later in this book for a definition of the 'without prejudice state'), once their reports have been exchanged. The order should incorporate a date by which simultaneous exchange of the reports will take place. Many arbitrators will make this date after the exchange of the statements of the witnesses of fact (see below).

Witnesses of fact are persons who provide evidence as to what has happened and confirmation that issues are as stated or as presented. These witnesses should be considered and the number on each side noted.

Such witnesses are distinguished from expert witnesses who provide evidence as to matters of opinion.

Simultaneous exchange of statements

In respect of these witnesses it should be noted that their statements should be ordered to be exchanged simultaneously.

Oaths and subpoenas

The arbitrator is vested with the power to administer the oath to witnesses but he has no power whatsoever to summon witnesses to appear before him.

COMPELLABILITY OF WITNESSES

Types of subpoena

Section 44 of the Arbitration Act 1996 gives the court the power to take the evidence of witnesses as it does in respect of legal proceedings. It therefore follows that the court is able to issue a *subpoena ad testificandum* or *subpoena duces tecum*.

A *subpoena ad testificandum* is an order to an individual that they should attend at the tribunal at the time and place specified to give evidence for the party who has issued the *subpoena*. The *subpoena duces tecum* is an order to an individual that he should bring specified documents to the tribunal. It should be noted that a person under *subpoena* to testify can be examined and cross-examined, whereas a person delivering documents under a *subpoena duces tecum* cannot be cross-examined on their contents.

Any party to the arbitration may apply to the local district registry of the High Court, Queen's Bench Division with an application or *praecipe*, and the court will issue the *subpoena* which must be personally served upon the witness, with an appropriate sum in conduct money. Service must be effected not later than 12 weeks after issue and not less than four days before the attendance is required.

The application is made by the party with the consent of the tribunal.

Forms of subpoena and procedure

The forms to be used are Form E20 Praecipe for Writ of Subpoena

Praecipe for Writ of Subpoena (Ord 38, r 14)

Title as in action

Seal a writ of subpoena   on behalf of the   directed to

Returnable

Dated the   day of   19

Signature of applicant

Accompanying the *Praecipe* should be a draft *Subpoena* in the following form. Upon receipt of this documentation the court will seal the *Subpoena* and it is then ready for service. There is no fee for the issue of such a *Subpoena*.

Forms G1 [*Subpoena ad Testificandum* (General Form)] and G2 [*Subpoena Duces Tecum*] are the relevant Forms for Writs of *Subpoena* (see below).

Form G1

Writ of Subpoena (Ord 38, r 14)

ELIZABETH THE SECOND, by the Grace of God, of the United Kingdom of Great Britain and Northern Ireland and of Our other realms and territories Queen, Head of the Commonwealth, Defender of the Faith.

To [names of witnesses]

We command you to attend at the sittings of the offices of   on   day of   at   for the Arbitration of the above named cause and from day to day thereafter until the end of the trial, to give evidence on behalf of

Witness,   Lord High Chancellor of Great Britain

the day of 19

Issued on day of 19

by

of

Solicitors for

Form G2

If the Writ is one of *Subpoena Duces Tecum*, the words AND WE ALSO COMMAND YOU to bring with you and produce at the place aforesaid on the day notified to you [here describe the documents or things to be produced].

Power of court to issue writ of habeas corpus

It is important to remember that the court has the inherent power to issue a writ of *habeas corpus*, ordering the production of a prisoner to the tribunal for the purposes of giving evidence.

Communication of the parties with the arbitrator

It is crucial that the arbitrator issues an order at the time of the preliminary meeting requiring the parties to ensure that any communication to him is simultaneously sent to the other party(ies).

MISCELLANEOUS ISSUES

Other matters which need to be dealt with at the preliminary hearing include whether or not the parties want a transcript or recording made of the hearing, and whether evidence will be taken under oath. The presumption is that it will be so. It is helpful to an arbitrator to have prior knowledge of any unusual religions as he may need to have particular 'Holy Books' such as the Adi Granth, Bhagavad Gita or Koran, which he may not usually carry. Even if he does not have an appropriate book the witness can affirm.

The reasoned award

A reasoned award is one in which the arbitrator effectively explains his decision. In England the Arbitration Act 1979 made the practice of providing such awards mandatory in the absence of an expressed agreement to the contrary. The Act gave the courts the power to remit an award for the purpose of allowing the arbitrator to insert his reasons. The purpose being that these would enable the court to decide whether the arbitrator had followed a proper course of reasoning in reaching his final decision, which led to the award in question.

The parties will need to decide whether they require a reasoned award.

It is the parties who decide whether or not the arbitrator should provide reasons when making his award. The arbitrator does not have the power to decide this.

Section 52 of the Arbitration Act makes it clear that the parties are free to make this decision and s 52(4) reads that the award shall contain the reasons for the award unless it is an agreed award or the parties have agreed to dispense with reasons.

The pre-trial hearing

The question as to whether the parties require a pre-trial hearing should be considered, and if required the date for it should be determined.

A date for the hearing should also be determined if it is possible at this time and an estimate of the number of days required for the hearing should be sought.

A preliminary note on the taxation of costs

The arbitrator can also address the question of the taxing of costs. The costs in an arbitration as in litigation are generally said to follow the event, ie: winner's costs are paid by the loser. Any agreement to the effect that one party will indemnify the other in respect of the costs of the arbitration will be void under s 60 of the Arbitration Act 1996, unless the agreement was made after the dispute in question arose. Sections 61–65 deal with the power of the Tribunal to deal with costs and the authority of the parties to determine how such costs are to be dealt with.

The arbitrator has the power to tax costs. More will be said of this later.

Once these matters have been determined the order made by the arbitrator can, and should, reflect as many of these issues as possible.

CHAPTER FIVE

ARBITRATION – THE PROCEEDINGS AND THE HEARING

THE PROCEEDINGS ARE THE VERY ESSENCE OF THE ARBITRATION

The Arbitration Act 1996 is very helpful to the arbitrator in that it confirms his powers in respect of the conduct of the proceedings. Much of the law is held in ss 33–41.

The relevant sections are as follows:

33 – (1) The tribunal shall –

(a) act fairly and impartially as between the parties, giving each party a reasonable opportunity of putting his case and dealing with that of his opponent; and

(b) adopt procedures suitable to the circumstances of the particular case, avoiding unnecessary delay or expense, so as to provide a fair means for the resolution of matters falling to be determined.

(2) The tribunal shall comply with that general duty in conducting the arbitral proceedings in its decisions on matters of procedure and evidence and in the exercise of all other powers conferred upon it.

34 – (1) It shall be for the tribunal to decide all procedural and evidential matters, subject to the right of the parties to agree any matter.

(2) Procedural and evidential matters include –

(a) when and where any part of the proceedings is to be held;

(b) the language or languages to be used in the proceedings and whether translations of any relevant documents are to be supplied;

(c) whether any and if so what form of written statements of claim and defence are to be used, when these should be supplied and the extent to which such statements can later be amended;

(d) whether any and if so what classes of documents should be disclosed between and produced by the parties and at what stage;

(e) whether any and if so what questions should be put to and answered by the respective parties and when and in what form this should be done;

(f) whether to apply strict rules of evidence (or any other rules) as to the admissibility, relevance or weight of any material (oral, written or other) sought to be tendered on any matters of fact or opinion and the time, manner and form in which such material should be exchanged and presented;

(g) whether and to what extent the tribunal should itself take the initiative in ascertaining the facts and the law;

(h) whether and to what extent there should be oral or written evidence or submissions.

(3) The tribunal may fix the time within which any directions given by it are to be complied with, and may if it thinks fit extend the time so fixed (whether or not it has expired).

35 – (1) The parties are free to agree –

(a) that the arbitral proceedings shall be consolidated with other arbitral proceedings; or

(b) that the concurrent hearings shall be held,

on such terms as may be agreed.

(2) Unless the parties agree to confer such power on the tribunal, the tribunal has no power to order consolidation of proceedings or concurrent hearings.

36 – Unless otherwise agreed by the parties, a party to an arbitral proceedings may be represented in the proceedings by a lawyer or other person chosen by him.

37 – (1) Unless otherwise agreed by the parties –

(a) the tribunal may –

(i) appoint experts or legal advisers to report to it and the parties; or

(ii) appoint assessors to assist it on technical matters, and may allow any such expert, legal adviser or assessor to attend the proceedings; and

(b) the parties shall be given a reasonable opportunity to comment on any information, opinion or advice offered by any such person.

(2) The fees and expenses of an expert, legal adviser or assessor appointed by the tribunal for which the arbitrators are liable are expenses of the arbitrators for the purpose of this Part.

38 – (1) The parties are free to agree on the powers exercisable by the arbitral tribunal for the purposes of and in relation to the proceedings.

(2) Unless otherwise agreed by the parties the tribunal has the following powers.

(3) The tribunal may order a claimant to provide security for the costs of the arbitration. This power shall not be exercised on the ground that the claimant is –

(a) an individual ordinarily resident outside the United Kingdom; or

(b) a corporation or association incorporated or formed under the law of a country outside the United Kingdom, or whose central management and control is exercised outside the United Kingdom.

(4) The tribunal may give directions in relation to any property which is the subject of the proceedings or as to which any question arises in the proceedings and which is owned by or is in the possession of a party to the proceedings –

(a) for the inspection, photographing, preservation, custody or detention of the property by the tribunal, an expert or a party; or

(b) ordering that samples be taken from, or any observation be made of or experiment conducted upon, the property.

(5) The tribunal may direct that a party or witness shall be examined on oath or affirmation, and for that purpose administer any necessary oath or take any necessary affirmation.

(6) The tribunal may give directions to a party for the preservation for the purposes of the proceedings of any evidence in his custody or control.

39 – (1) The parties are free to agree that the tribunal shall have power to order on a provisional basis any relief which it would have the power to grant in a final award.

(2) This includes, for instance, making –

(a) a provisional order for the payment of money or the disposition of property as between the parties; or

(b) an order to make an interim payment on account of the costs of the arbitration.

(3) Any such order shall be subject to the tribunal's final adjudication; and the tribunal's final award, on the merits or as to costs, shall take account of any such order.

(4) Unless the parties agree to confer such power on the tribunal, the tribunal has no such power. This does not affect its powers under section 47 (awards on different issues &c).

40 – (1) The Parties shall do all things necessary for the proper and expeditious conduct of the arbitral proceedings.

(2) This includes –

(a) complying without delay with any determination of the tribunal as to procedural or evidential matters, or with any order or directions of the tribunal; and

(b) where appropriate, taking without delay any necessary steps to obtain a decision of the court on a preliminary question of jurisdiction or law (see sections 32 and 45).

41 – (1) The parties are free to agree on the powers of the tribunal in case of a party's failure to do something necessary for the proper and expeditious conduct of the arbitration.

(2) Unless otherwise agreed by the parties, the following provisions apply.

(3) If the tribunal is satisfied that there has been inordinate and inexcusable delay on the part of the claimant in pursuing his claim and that the delay –

(a) gives rise, or is likely to give rise to a substantial risk that it is not possible to have a fair resolution of the issues in that claim; or

(b) has caused, or is likely to cause, serious prejudice to the respondent,

the tribunal may make an award dismissing the claim.

(4) If without showing sufficient cause a party –

(a) fails to attend or be represented at an oral hearing of which due notice was given; or

(b) where matters are to be dealt with in writing, fails after due notice to submit written evidence or make written submissions,

the tribunal may continue the proceedings in the absence of that party or, as the case may be, without any written evidence or submissions on his behalf, and may make an award on the basis of evidence before it.

(5) If without showing sufficient cause a party fails to comply with any order or directions of the tribunal, the tribunal may make a peremptory order to the same effect, prescribing such time for compliance with it as the tribunal considers appropriate.

(6) If a claimant fails to comply with a peremptory order of the tribunal to provide security for costs, the tribunal may make an award dismissing his claim.

(7) If a party fails to comply with any other kind of peremptory order, then, without prejudice to section 42 (enforcement by court of tribunal's peremptory orders), the tribunal may do any of the following –

(a) direct that the party in default shall not be entitled to rely upon any allegation or material which was the subject matter of the order;

(b) draw such inferences from the non-compliance as circumstances justify;

(c) proceed to an award on the basis of such materials as have been properly provided to it;

(d) make such order as it thinks fit as to the payment of costs of the arbitration incurred in consequence of the non-compliance.

COMMENT UPON THE PARTIES' POWERS

Section 38 of the Arbitration Act 1996 is of major consequence and a very significant advance over the earlier Acts. It provides the parties with the power to define the powers they wish to vest the arbitrator with, and in default of such agreement, specifies the powers which the arbitrator will be deemed to have. Later sections provide for judicial control of these powers but it is clear from the Act that Parliament intended to and has strengthened the position of the arbitrator very significantly.

THE PAYMENT INTO COURT

One matter which has not been adequately dealt with in arbitrations as opposed to litigation is the payment into court. This is the means by which a party can attempt to reduce his liability to costs.

A party makes a payment into court representing what he considers equates to an estimation of reasonable damages. If this is made and the other party accepts it, the dispute is at an end. If, however, it is rejected its significance is that, should an equal or lesser amount be awarded at the conclusion of the hearing then costs incurred after the time the payment was made will not be awarded against the respondent except in exceptional circumstances.

THE SEALED OFFER

In arbitrations the nearest that is usually possible is the sealed offer. The sealed offer is a written offer made to the other party to pay such a sum as is thought reasonable.

Effect of payment into court or sealed offer

The importance of the payment into court or the sealed offer is that the arbitrator does not know that the offer has been made. Thus his final determination cannot be influenced by such an admission.

A NOVEL SYSTEM OF DEALING WITH THE OFFER

A slight refinement of the whole can be made whereby the parties can make the equivalent of a sealed offer but can 'back it' with money paid to an independent stakeholder on the same terms as would apply to a payment into court. This gives the other party the confidence that there is money behind the offer. There is inevitably a small administrative charge made by the stakeholder, a solicitor, but despite the charge it is a satisfactory alternative to the simple written offer.

THE HEARING

The hearing is the culmination of the parties' preparation and is the time at which their attention to detail and choice of arbitrator will pay dividends or cost the earth.

Where should the arbitration be held?

The location of the hearing is of importance. It should be on neutral territory, that is it should not be in the offices of either party and should be held on premises where there is privacy and relative comfort. It should be remembered that witnesses will probably be kept waiting and there may be a need for advocates to conduct interviews with their clients or witnesses. In addition, it may be necessary for advocates to hold discussions between themselves and if all this is not possible the actual proceedings can be jeopardised.

The ideal premises

Suitable premises can range from an office complex to a hotel. In choosing the premises one should be mindful of the fact that charges will be made and in a few cases the proceedings may last for some weeks.

Each party will require a room to which they can retire with their legal advisers and others.

How to set up the room for a hearing

The main room should be capable of holding a horseshoe of tables with each limb being long enough to comfortably accommodate one side.

The arbitrator will sit at the top on the cross bench.

There should be room for a chair between the cross benches facing the arbitrator where the witnesses will sit and give evidence.

ARBITRATOR SHOULD NEVER BE COMPROMISED

Purely as a matter of obvious comment, the arbitrator should ensure that at no point in the period between his appointment and the conclusion of the proceedings is his position compromised, which can easily occur in a hotel should one party offer him a drink or sit at the same table. Any contact with one party should always be in the presence of the other party or their representative, and then only in the course of duties connected with the arbitration itself.

FORM OF PROCEEDINGS

It is assumed that an arbitrator will conduct the proceedings in an adversarial manner, which is the accepted form of litigation within the courts. It is worth noting however that there is in fact nothing to prevent the parties requiring the arbitrator to conduct the proceedings in an inquisitorial manner. Before an arbitrator decided to invoke this form of procedure he would do well to ensure that the parties understood the meaning of the form of words and that they were totally clear and adamant that it was the inquisitorial approach that was desired.

The inquisitorial approach is accepted as procedure in many if not most tribunals under the influence of Roman law. This means that in most continental countries it is the accepted format. However, in the English jurisdiction it has no place in most of the state tribunals, a notable exception being the Coroner's Court.

The claimant's opening and progress

The proceedings will be commenced with an opening address from the claimant or his advocate. This will be followed by the advocate calling his witnesses one at a time. Each witness will take the oath or, if he prefers or circumstances dictate, an affirmation. After this he will be led through his evidence in chief by his advocate and then subjected to the tender mercies of the other side's advocate who will cross-examine him. Following this, the claimant's advocate will have a chance to re-examine his witness, putting to him questions to clarify any issues that arose during the cross-examination.

He may also introduce evidence by way of affidavit or other evidence such as photographs, documents, computer records and video recordings.

Authority of arbitrator to administer the oath

The authority of the arbitrator to administer the oath derives from the Arbitration Act 1996 s 38 which, compared to s 12 of the Arbitration Act 1950, provides much greater default powers to the arbitrator, and, consequently, there will be considerably less need to apply to the court for powers in default of agreement by the parties. Section 38 is reproduced above.

The other relevant Act is the Oaths Act 1978. Section 1 of this Act directs the manner in which an oath may be administered. Section 5 of the Act permits the administration of a solemn affirmation, s 5(1), to any person objecting to being sworn whilst s 5(2) allows the administration of the solemn affirmation to any person to whom it is not practical to administer the oath.

Arbitrator unable to summon witness

The arbitrator has absolutely no power to summon a witness and only the party to an arbitration is vested with that power (see above).

Arbitrator can question the witness

The arbitrator will have a chance to ask any questions he has of the witness.

He should restrict his questions to matters which have previously arisen during the witness's own evidence. If any new issues are raised, both parties' advocates must be given a chance to pursue matters with further questions.

The respondent

The process is the same until each of the claimant's witnesses have been heard and then the respondent pursues a similar course of action through his witnesses.

Finalising the hearing

After all the witnesses have been heard, there will be closing speeches, first from the claimant and then the respondent.

Following this, the arbitrator will normally close the proceedings and leave to consider his findings.

CHAPTER SIX

THE AWARD

The award is the arbitrator's judgment and it is important that it be clear and unambiguous. It must be certain in nature and capable of enforcement.

The arbitrator's award is the means by which he informs the parties of his decision. It should be in writing and should, unless a wish to the contrary has been expressed by the parties, be a reasoned award. This means that it contains the arbitrator's reasoning in so far as it allows the reader to understand what findings he has made and what conclusions he has reached, to include his decisions as to how the matter should be resolved and what money he has directed should be paid and to whom, together with a calculation of interest due.

Usually the decision will be a financial award but it is also possible that the arbitrator will order specific performance. An example of this being the dissolution of a partnership, in a case where a partnership dispute is being subjected to arbitration.

It is important that his conclusions are clear and unequivocal.

Having drafted his award he will sign it and date it.

In order to appreciate the way in which an award may be drafted there follows a skeleton draft award:

A   The arbitration agreement: date and parties

B   Date and method of appointment of arbitrator

C   The procedure adopted (documents only; or if hearing, give dates)

D   The issues

E   First issue of fact: I find as a fact that ...... because the evidence of Mr X was more closely supported by the contemporaneous documents than that of Mr Y or I preferred the evidence of Mr Z to that of Mr A or as appropriate

F   The first issue of law:

Argument for claimant .....

Argument for respondent .....

I prefer the case of the .... because

(1).......

(2).......

I therefore find for the ...... on this issue

G   Second issue (as first)

I therefore find for the ..... on this issue

H   I therefore determine and award ..... with interest at .... per cent from ...... to (the date of this award or, as the case may be, ... cent from ...)

J   (i) This award is final as to all matters except costs

(ii) If either party wishes to make representations to me as to costs, it should send them to me, and to the other party, by noon on ...... If either party wishes to make any representations in answer to the other party's representations, it should send them to me, and to the other party, by noon on .... Thereafter I will make my final award

K   I AWARD AND DETERMINE that the .... shall pay to the .... the costs of this arbitration to be taxed (if not agreed) [by me] OR [in the High Court].

His award will eventually be published and in the interest of justice his consideration should be as expedient as possible.

The very powerful benefits to all the parties of proceedings being held in confidence and of the issues being determined by a technically competent person cannot be overstated.

AWARD OF COSTS

The award may address the question of costs and provide as part of the award an order in respect of costs.

It was stated earlier that s 60 of the Arbitration Act 1996 restricted the ability of the parties to make prior agreement as to how the costs should be dealt with.

Sections 61–65 of the Arbitration Act 1996

Sections 61–65 of the Arbitration Act 1996 address the matter of costs:

61 – (1) The tribunal may make an award allocating the costs of the arbitration as between the parties, subject to any agreement of the parties.

(2) Unless the parties otherwise agree, the tribunal shall award costs on the general principle that costs should follow the event except where it appears to the tribunal that in the circumstances this is not appropriate in relation to the whole or part of the costs.

63 – (1) The parties are free to agree what costs of the arbitration are recoverable.

(2) If or to the extent there is no such agreement, the following provisions apply.

(3) The tribunal may determine by award the recoverable costs of the arbitration on such basis as it thinks fit.

If it does so it shall specify –

(a) the basis on which it has acted; and

(b) the items of recoverable costs and the amount referable to each.

(4) If the tribunal does not determine the recoverable costs of the arbitration, any party to the arbitral proceedings may apply to the court (upon notice to the other parties) which may –

(a) determine the recoverable costs of the arbitration on such basis as it thinks fit; or

(b) order that they shall be determined by such means and upon such terms as it may specify.

(5) Unless the tribunal or the court determines otherwise –

(a) the recoverable costs of the arbitration shall be determined on the basis that there shall be allowed a reasonable amount in respect of all costs reasonably incurred; and

(b) any doubt as to whether costs were reasonably incurred or were reasonable in amount shall be resolved in favour of the paying party.

(6) The above provisions have effect subject to section 64 (recoverable fees and expenses of arbitrators).

(7) Nothing in this section affects any right of the arbitrators, any expert, legal adviser or assessor appointed by the tribunal, or arbitral institution, to payment of their fees and expenses.

64 – (1) Unless otherwise agreed by the parties, the recoverable costs of the arbitration shall include in respect of the fees and expenses of the arbitrators only such reasonable fees and expenses as are appropriate in the circumstances.

(2) If there is any question as to what reasonable fees and expenses are appropriate in the circumstances, and the matter is not already before the court on application under section 63(4), the court may on the application of any party (upon notice to the other parties) –

(a) determine the matter; or

(b) order that it be determined by such means and upon such terms as the court may specify.

(3) Subsection (1) has effect subject to any order of the court under sections 24(4) or 25(3)(b) (order as to entitlement to fees or expenses in case of removal or resignation of arbitrator).

(4) Nothing in this section affects any right of the arbitrator to payment of his fees and expenses.

65 – (1) Unless otherwise agreed by the parties, the tribunal may direct that the recoverable costs of the arbitration, or any part of the arbitral proceedings, shall be limited to a specified amount.

(2) Any direction may be made or varied at any stage, but this must be done sufficiently in advance of the incurring of costs to which it relates, or the taking of any steps in the proceedings which may be affected by it, for the limit to be taken into account.

DERIVATION OF THE ARBITRATOR'S POWER TO AWARD COSTS

Section 49 Arbitration Act 1996

The tribunal has the power to award costs and this power derives from the agreement of the parties and the Arbitration Act 1996, under s 49, which reads:

49 – (1) The parties are free to agree on the powers of the tribunal as regards the award of interest.

(2) Unless otherwise agreed by the parties the following provisions apply.

(3) The tribunal may award simple or compound interest from such dates, at such rates and with such rests as it considers meets the justice of the case –

(a) on the whole or part of any amount awarded by the tribunal, in respect of any period up to the date of the award;

(b) on the whole or part of any amount claimed in the arbitration and outstanding at the commencement of the arbitral proceedings but paid before the award was made, in respect of any period up to the date of payment.

(4) The tribunal may award simple or compound interest from the date of the award (or any later date) until payment, at such rates and with such rests as it considers meets the justice of the case, on the outstanding amount of any award (including any award of interest under subsection (3) and any award as to costs).

(5) References in this section to an amount awarded by the tribunal include an amount payable in consequence of a declaratory award by the tribunal.

(6) The above provisions do not affect any other power of the tribunal to award interest.

POWER OF COURTS TO ENFORCE AWARD

As previously discussed the award, which should be in writing and signed by the arbitrator, is of much legal significance as it may be enforced through the courts.

The award can be enforced through the courts (Rules of Supreme Court Ord 73 r 10) and s 66 of the Arbitration Act 1996.

Section 66 Arbitration Act 1996

66 – (1) An award made by the tribunal pursuant to an arbitration agreement may, by leave of the court, be enforced in the same manner as a judgment or order of the court to the same effect.

(2) Where leave is so given, judgment may be entered in terms of the award.

(3) Leave to enforce an award shall not be given where, or to the extent that the person against whom it is sought to be enforced shows that the tribunal lacked substantive jurisdiction to make the award.

The right to raise such an objection may have been lost (see s 73).

(4) Nothing in this section affects the recognition or enforcement of an award under any other enactment or rule of law, in particular under Part II of the Arbitration Act 1950 (enforcement of awards under the Geneva Convention) or the provisions of Part III of this Act relating to the recognition and enforcement of awards under the New York Convention or by action on the award.

POWER OF COURT TO SET ASIDE AN AWARD

Equally, application can be made to the court to set aside the award on a number of grounds.

Section 67 Arbitration Act 1996

67 – (1) A party to arbitral proceedings may (upon notice to the other parties and to the tribunal) apply to the court –

> (a) challenging any award of the arbitral tribunal as to its substantive jurisdiction; or

> (b) for an order declaring an award made by the tribunal on the merits to be of no effect, in whole or in part, because the tribunal did not have substantive jurisdiction.

A party may lose the right to object (see section 73) and the right to apply is subject to the restrictions in section 70(2) and (3).

(2) The arbitral tribunal may continue the arbitral proceedings and make a further award while an application to the court under this section is pending in relation to an award as to its jurisdiction.

(3) On application under this section challenging an award of the arbitral tribunal as to its substantive jurisdiction, the court may by order –

> (a) confirm the award;

> (b) vary the award; or

> (c) set aside the award in whole or in part.

(4) The leave of the court is required for any appeal from a decision of the court under this section.

68 – (1) A party to arbitral proceedings may (upon notice to the other parties and to the tribunal) apply to the court challenging an award in the proceedings on the ground of serious irregularity affecting the tribunal, the proceedings or the award.

A party may lose this right to object (see section 73) and the right to apply is subject to the restriction in section 70(2) and (3).

(2) Serious irregularity means an irregularity of one or more of the following kinds which the court considers has caused or will cause substantial injustice to the applicant –

(a) failure by the tribunal to comply with section 33 (general duty of tribunal);

(b) the tribunal exceeding its powers (otherwise than by exceeding its substantive jurisdiction: see section 67);

(c) failure by the tribunal to conduct the proceedings in accordance with the procedure agreed by the parties;

(d) failure by the tribunal to deal with all the issues that were put to it;

(e) any arbitral or other institution or person vested by the parties with powers in relation to the proceedings or the award exceeding its powers;

(f) uncertainty or ambiguity as to the effect of the award;

(g) the award being obtained by fraud or the award or the way in which it was procured being contrary to public policy;

(h) failure to comply with the requirements as to the form of the award; or

(i) any irregularity in the conduct of the proceedings or in the award which is admitted by the tribunal or by any arbitral or other institution or person vested by the parties with powers in relation to the proceedings or the award.

(3) If there is shown serious irregularity affecting the tribunal, the proceedings or the award, the court may –

(a) remit the award to the tribunal, in whole or in part, for reconsideration;

(b) set the award aside in whole or in part; or

(c) declare the award to be of no effect, in whole or in part.

The court shall not exercise its power to set aside or to declare an award to be of no effect, in whole or in part, unless it is satisfied that it would be inappropriate to remit the matters in question to the tribunal for reconsideration.

(4) Leave of the court is required for any appeal from a decision of the court under this section.

69 – (1) Unless otherwise agreed by the parties, a party to arbitral proceedings may (upon notice to the other parties and to the tribunal) appeal to the court on a question of law arising out of an award made in the proceedings.

An agreement to dispense with reasons for the tribunal's award shall be considered an agreement to exclude the court's jurisdiction under this section.

(2) An appeal shall not be brought under this section except –

(a) with the agreement of all the other parties to the proceedings; or

(b) with the leave of the court.

The right to appeal is also subject to the restriction in section 70(2) and (3).

(3) Leave to appeal shall be given only if the court is satisfied –

(a) that the determination of the question will substantially affect the rights of one or more of the parties;

(b) that the question is one which the tribunal was asked to determine;

(c) that on the basis of the findings of fact in the award –

(i) the decision of the tribunal on the question is obviously wrong; or

(ii) the question is one of general public importance and the decision of the tribunal is at least open to serious doubt; and

(d) that, despite the agreement of the parties to resolve the matter by arbitration, it is just and proper in all the circumstances for the court to determine the question.

(4) An application for leave to appeal under this section shall identify the question of law to be determined and state the grounds on which it is alleged that leave to appeal should be granted.

(5) The court shall determine an application for leave to appeal under this section without a hearing unless it appears to the court that a hearing is required.

(6) The leave of the court is required for any appeal from a decision of the court under this section to grant or refuse leave to appeal.

(7) On appeal under this section the court may by order –

(a) confirm the award;

(b) vary the award;

(c) remit the award to the tribunal, in whole or in part, for reconsideration in the light of the court's determination; or

(d) set aside the award in whole or in part.

The court shall not exercise its power to set aside an award, in whole or in part, unless it is satisfied that it would be inappropriate to remit the matters in question to the tribunal for reconsideration.

(8) The decision of the court on an appeal under this section shall be treated as a judgment of the court for the purposes of a further appeal.

But no such appeal lies without the leave of the court which shall not be given unless the court considers that the question is of general importance or one which for some other special reason should be considered by the Court of Appeal.

OBJECTION OF A PARTY TO THE PROCEEDINGS

One aspect of law which has been radically adjusted by the Arbitration Act 1996 is the 'codification' of the right or otherwise of a party to an arbitration agreement to object to proceedings. This is enshrined in s 73. There has always been a general assumption in arbitration proceedings that a party who does not object to anything and who allows it to proceed is by consent waiving his right to later lodge an objection to it. It has, however, not been a principle with established certainty.

Section 73 of the Arbitration Act 1996 now covers this issue and is reproduced below for the benefit of the reader.

Section 73 Arbitration Act 1996

73 – (1) If a party to arbitral proceedings takes part, or continues to take part, in the proceedings without making, either forthwith or within such time as is allowed by the arbitration agreement or the tribunal or by any provision of this Part, any objection –

(a) that the tribunal lacks substantive jurisdiction;

(b) that the proceedings have been improperly conducted;

(c) that there has been a failure to comply with the arbitration agreement or with any provision of this Part; or

(d) that there has been any other irregularity affecting the tribunal or the proceedings,

he may not raise that objection later, before the tribunal or the court, unless he shows that, at the time he took part or continued to take part in the proceedings, he did not know and could not with reasonable diligence have discovered the grounds for the objection.

(2) Where the arbitral tribunal rules that it has substantive jurisdiction and a party to arbitral proceedings who could have questioned that ruling –

(a) by any available arbitral process of appeal or review; or

(b) by challenging the award,

does not do so, or does not do so within the time allowed by the arbitration agreement or any provision of this Part, he may not object later to the tribunal's substantive jurisdiction on any ground which was the subject to that ruling.

CHAPTER SEVEN

MEDIATION

Mediation is the name given to a variety of procedures which can be used to resolve disputes without recourse to the courts. The group of procedures known generically as mediation allow parties to disputes to resolve them and remain in an equitable relationship.

INTRODUCTORY COMMENTS

The subject of mediation is not generally well understood by lawyers. Those who know nothing about it fear it because it seems to take control of the case away from them. This, as will be seen later, is a myth. Some lawyers may fear it because it may result in a settlement of the case, an obviously undesirable situation because, once a case is settled, its potential to earn them fees evaporates.

A competent lawyer should, however, consider the quick resolution of the dispute to be to his immediate and long-term benefit.

A party whose lawyer is reluctant to settle a case should discuss the matter carefully with his lawyer and, if it becomes obvious that there is a marked reluctance to discuss matters with the other party, he should ask whether or not he has instructed the best man.

MEDIATION – A WITHOUT PREJUDICE PROCESS

Mediation is effectively a 'without prejudice' process, whereby the parties to a dispute are assisted by a neutral third party to resolve the dispute on terms which hopefully all will find acceptable.

Before proceeding with this chapter, it is important for the reader to have some understanding of the 'without prejudice' status.

The courts will take evidence, in whatever form is appropriate, from any witness who appears before it or has submitted evidence to it.

Although not strictly a matter for discussion under the heading of mediation, the 'without prejudice' status requires some explanation. Some of this paragraph is more applicable to the chapter on arbitration and should be read with this in mind.

The preferred way in which evidence is taken is orally where the witness is sworn and the other parties have an opportunity to test the evidence by means of cross-examination. Other ways of submitting evidence include the use of *affidavits,* which are sworn written statements. These have the disadvantage of not allowing the evidence to be tested by the parties. There are ways of getting around this problem but these methods are not within the scope of this book. There will be some further discussion in the chapters on arbitration.

THE WITHOUT PREJUDICE STATE

It is fundamental to the court system that all persons can be compelled to give evidence, subject to certain restrictions. The restrictions relate to a number of factors, including incompetence by way of age and mental ability, public interest, without prejudice privilege and professional privilege.

Without prejudice privilege

In the context of mediation, it is the 'without prejudice' privilege which is of importance. The courts have accepted since the last century that, in the interests of due legal process, negotiations between the parties which are aimed at resolving the dispute should be given a special status namely that, these negotiations should be encouraged. Thus the doctrine of 'without prejudice' evolved.

In *Walker v Wilsher* (1889), the original doctrine was born. The rule was reconfirmed in the case of *Rush & Tomkins v GLC* (1988). In this case there was considerable discussion of the 'without prejudice' status and it was stated that there were considerable misconceptions as to the actual status. The original rule set out in *Walker v Wilsher* was reconfirmed.

Principles of the process

The Court of Appeal in *Rush & Tomkins v GLC* set out six principles as to how the doctrine would operate. These were:

- The purpose of 'without prejudice' privilege was to enable the parties to negotiate without risk of their proposals being used against them if the negotiations failed. Once a settlement had been agreed, the privilege was revoked. It was noted that such privilege existed whether the claim for it was against the other party or someone outside the party.
- It was confirmed that the parties could mutually agree to refer to such discussion or correspondence even if a settlement had not been reached.

- It was possible for the parties to use a special form of words which at least between themselves precluded reference to the correspondence even after settlement had been reached.
- It was stated that the privilege did not depend upon the existence of proceedings.
- The courts could always determine, after considering a document, whether the privilege applied to it.
- The privilege extended to the solicitors of the parties to the 'without prejudice' negotiations.

PROFESSIONAL PRIVILEGE

The doctrine of professional privilege applies to the advantage of a client who has the right to claim privilege in respect of communications with his legal adviser relating to the proceedings. The privilege is that of the client and not of the lawyer.

It was further stated that details of a 'without prejudice' settlement was, and remained, privileged and that it could not be used in court proceedings against the parties by a third party.

The 'without prejudice' nature of the process means that the parties can explore means of resolving the issues without committing themselves to anything until they are agreeable to doing so.

THE BENEFITS

The benefit of this means of resolving a dispute is that the parties can agree to resolve the matter in a way which would not be possible through a court which must of necessity give a ruling which correctly reflects the law and the terms of any contract.

In discussion with lawyers involved in personal injury cases and with medical negligence cases, it is not infrequently said that the objections to mediation include the fact that nothing can be done until the case is ready for trial and then one might as well go to trial. Since only the smallest number of cases ever reach trial, it can be seen that this approach is not realistic and delays the almost inevitable settlement.

It is of interest that in a recent publication of eminent lawyers from the United States of America, the topic was aired to the extent that a whole journal was devoted to mediation.

The reasons for not using mediation were dealt with in some considerable detail and included reasons such as:

Do you or your client, the insurance adjuster or the other attorney need a reality check?

Mediation cannot work because the mediator does not wear a black gown and have a gavel to beat the parties into submission. Mediation does not require, and indeed suffers if it is treated as a court hearing before, a judge.

It is not until this method is considered that the benefits become obvious. Those objecting to it usually do so from a position of ignorance or self-benefit.

In most cases the dispute will be such that the parties are emotionally involved and to some extent are unwilling to give way.

When to mediate

The decision to go to mediation may be taken at any time from the moment a dispute arises until the moment before a judge hands down a ruling.

The only decision the parties need take is that mediation might be appropriate to their particular dispute. Having made such a decision and agreed upon it between themselves, they will need to appoint a mediator.

Before doing so, it is perhaps relevant to discuss the way in which mediation can be funded. The trend within the courts is to encourage mediation and it has certainly become very fashionable to talk in terms of using it but, until funding is clarified, there is little hope of it becoming a useful means of resolving disputes.

THE OPTIONS

What are the options

If it is assumed that the disputes under discussion are those between a doctor and his patient, or a health authority and a patient, or an injured party and an insurance company, then one party will usually have a significant financial advantage over the other.

Despite the legal system encouraging the parties to a dispute to go to mediation, there has been little financial incentive for them to do so.

The costing

The trials of mediation which have already taken place have almost invariably relied upon the mediator working *pro bono publico*, a situation which should not and must not be allowed to continue.

Legal Aid

It is a fact that the current Legal Aid restrictions are designed to reduce the cost of litigation to the public purse and thus it can be assumed that there is very little chance of a legally aided person receiving funding from the authority for such a process.

Who should fund it

The question therefore arises as to how the process can and should be funded.

It should be remembered that it is implicit in the appointment of a mediator that he is independent of all parties to the dispute. It is thus unhelpful if he is in the pay of one of the parties.

There are a number of ways of overcoming these difficulties:

The telephone mediation

If the case is to be dealt with by means of mediation by telephone, only a few telephone calls and letters are involved so the payment by the commissioning party should not result in any problems.

It is when the case progresses and takes longer to conclude that the relationship between the original commissioning party and the mediator becomes significant.

The legally aided party

As previously mentioned, Legal Aid will not cover the costs of mediation and if lawyers are acting under a Legal Aid Certificate, the insurer against whom they are acting will usually offer an indemnity in respect of the mediation and mediator's fees, provided that this is not made known to the mediator. However, it is almost a legal fiction that his independence is not compromised.

The insurer's indemnity

By providing the indemnity, the insurer, in a case where the other party is legally aided, protects his position since he would not be able to obtain an order for costs even if he were to be exonerated.

Who should mediate the medical dispute

How to find such a person does require some care. The parties would benefit from the person being a qualified mediator and, whilst it is not essential that he or she should be knowledgeable of the medical sphere, there is some advantage in having a person whose knowledge of the field is substantial.

Where to find a suitable person

There are a number of sources from which the appropriate person can be sought including Dispute Resolution Services Ltd. Sources include the Chartered Institute of Arbitrators, who maintain a list of persons holding appropriate qualification as mediators, as do the Centre for Dispute Resolution and many trade organisations also maintain such lists as do the various other qualifying bodies in the United Kingdom.

Having found a suitable person

Having decided upon a suitable person he should be approached and, assuming that he is willing, appointed to the post.

THE ATTITUDE OF THE LAW

A feature which would be most welcome in English law is for the present 'without prejudice' status to be fully confirmed in law.

Whilst it can be expected that the courts will, as a matter of public policy, rule to the benefit of the technique, treating it as 'without prejudice' negotiations is no guarantee that this will occur either generally or in the individual case, since the only real support for the technique in England is the Practice Direction of January 1994, with some additional support from later Practice Directions.

High Court procedure

The present High Court Form B90 Pre Trial Check List requires the solicitor to answer three questions concerning Alternative Dispute Resolution. These are:

- Have you or counsel discussed with your client(s) the possibility of attempting to resolve the dispute (or particular issues) by ADR?
- Might some form of ADR procedure assist to resolve or narrow the issues in this case?
- Have you or your client(s) explored with the other parties the possibility of resolving this dispute (or particular issues) by ADR?

Put in this form, they can be readily dealt with by a solicitor or party with no intention of submitting the dispute to mediation.

The Practice Direction (49) made by Master Foster at the beginning of November 1996, strengthens this early attempt to force ADR on parties to litigation. See Order 5(c) of the Direction, which introduces sanction to reluctant parties.

The authority of the mediator

The appointment of a mediator gives no authority to that person unlike the appointment of an arbitrator. He holds no authority to impose a resolution and indeed the parties will not receive a solution from him. His task is to encourage and cajole the parties into making decisions.

The immunity of the mediator

It is also important to remember that the mediator has no immunity from being sued for negligence and, although the possibilities are limited, bearing in mind the parties are in contention, it is not impossible that allegations will be raised even if later disproved. An allegation of breach of confidence leading to a material loss could, without doubt, cause the mediator much loss of time and expense.

PROFESSIONAL INDEMNITY INSURANCE

It is therefore important to ensure that the appointed person carries a reasonable level of indemnity insurance.

In appointing that person it would be reasonable for the parties to enquire as to whether such indemnity was in force.

The cost of such a policy is small, as is the risk, but the importance of having it is something no mediator should practise unless he has considered obtaining it. No party should appoint a mediator unless he can be reassured that such a policy is in existence.

Policies providing indemnity for mediators are readily available and the premiums are relatively minimal.

A COMMENT UPON THE VOLUNTEERS IN COMMUNITY SERVICE

This comment also applies to those who undertake mediation in the community and under the auspices of such bodies as the Citizens' Advice Bureaux.

THE STRENGTHS OF THE PROCESS

The strength of the process is the fact that either party can walk out of a mediation at any time and thus the skill of the mediator is to keep the parties together.

TECHNIQUES OF MEDIATING

There are as many methods of mediating a dispute as there are viruses causing mild illnesses in the population. For the purposes of this chapter, only two significant types will be mentioned and of these only one will be discussed in any considerable depth.

Because the differences in technique are so many, this chapter will reflect the author's own experience and methods. What follows is a description of some of the benefits by means of examples of disputes.

HAVING APPOINTED THE MEDIATOR

Having nominated the mediator, he will probably invite the parties to agree his fees and then he will ensure that they fully understand the nature of the process. The contract and schedule provide the parties with a full explanation of the method and a copy of a contract is reproduced below.

THE CONTRACTUAL AGREEMENT

AGREEMENT TO MEDIATION
1. The following disputes have arisen between the parties.
2. The disputants have agreed to request the mediator to accept the appointment as mediator for the settlement of these disputes.
3. The disputants have agreed that the mediator should conduct the mediation in accordance with the attached guidelines.

This DEED is made on   between the disputants and the mediator both named below.

IT IS AGREED
1. The mediator accepts the appointment and agrees to conduct the mediation in accordance with the attached guidelines for mediation.
2. The disputants hereby agree that should any disputant notify the mediator

that he wishes to terminate the mediation or that the mediator should decide that a resolution is unlikely, then the said disputant or the mediator, as appropriate, shall give notice to the other disputants and the mediator, if appropriate, that the mediation be concluded.

3. The disputants bind themselves jointly and severally to pay upon demand the mediator's fees and disbursements in accordance with the rates set out in the attached Schedule. The disputants between themselves settle all costs of the mediation in accordance with the guidelines.

4. The disputants agree that they will jointly and severally indemnify the mediator, against all claims, demands, proceedings, damages, costs, charges and expenses which may arise in connection with or arising out of the mediation, or the way in which it is conducted and will not themselves bring any such claim against the mediator.

SIGNED AS A DEED AND WITNESSED

First Disputant

(Name)

(Signature)

(Address)

(Date)

IN THE PRESENCE OF:

(Name)

(Address)

Second Disputant

(Name)

(Signature)

(Address)

(Date)

IN THE PRESENCE OF:

(Name)

(Address)

Third Disputant

(Name)

(Signature)

(Address)

(Date)

IN THE PRESENCE OF:

(Name)

(Address)

Fourth Disputant

(Name)

(Signature)

(Address)

(Date)

IN THE PRESENCE OF:

(Name)

(Address)

(Name)

Mediator

IN THE PRESENCE OF:

(Name)

(Address)

AGREEMENT TO MEDIATE APPLICATION No:
SCHEDULE TO THE AGREEMENT TO MEDIATION

THE MEDIATOR'S FEE: The mediator will be paid at the rate of £   per hour with a minimum fee of £   . Time spent by the mediator in travelling will be charged at   % of the hourly fee.

DISBURSEMENTS: The mediator will charge at cost any disbursements properly made in respect of:

(a) Telephone calls, faxes and other forms of communication.

(b) Postage and any delivery charges.

(c) Travelling, hotel expenses, and similar expenses.

(d) Accommodation and other expenses relating to the venue for the mediation session.

(e) Mileage will be charged at per mile.

(f) Any taxes such as VAT which are required to be charged by law will be added to the above charges as is appropriate.

The mediator will be entitled to receive payment for disbursements, in advance of incurring them, from any party. The party who pays any such sum to the mediator will be able to recover an equal share of such payment from the other parties to the dispute as a debt due.

SPECIAL TERMS
GUIDELINES TO MEDIATION

INTRODUCTION: Mediation is a process whereby a dispute between two or more persons or companies is resolved by remitting the dispute to a private hearing before an independent neutral third party (the mediator), whose role is to assist the parties in reaching a mutually satisfactory solution to the matters in dispute. The mediator may not impose a settlement on the parties.

THE MEDIATOR: Unless specified otherwise, the term 'the mediator', within the context of these guidelines shall be read as _____ (name of mediator).

USE OF THE GUIDELINES: Unless otherwise specified by the parties, these guidelines shall be deemed to be part of the parties' agreement to mediate, although the parties may by agreement vary these guidelines.

CONFIRMATION OF MEDIATOR: The mediator shall not embark upon the mediation without the written approval of the parties to the dispute which is to be mediated. Before such approval is given, the mediator shall disclose to the parties any interest he may have in the dispute or with any of the parties, and any other circumstances likely to affect the presumption of impartiality.

MEETING OF THE PARTIES WITH THE MEDIATOR: As soon as is practicable (and in any event within two weeks) after his appointment, the mediator will arrange a meeting before him of all the parties to the dispute. The mediator will fix the date, time, and venue of the meeting. The mediator may request further details of the facts or issues from the parties. At least seven days before the meeting, each party to the dispute may provide the mediator with a brief memorandum setting out the relevant facts and issues in the dispute, and their position on these issues. The mediator may send the memorandum to the other parties. Prior to the meeting, the parties should not forward any other documents to the mediator, unless at his specific request. If necessary, the mediator may, with the agreement of the parties, visit any place relevant to the dispute, or seek legal or other advice. On any visit, the mediator should be accompanied by a representative of all the parties.

CONDUCT OF THE MEETING: The parties should bring to the meeting all documents and information which they may wish to bring to the attention of the mediator. At the meeting, the mediator may hold joint or separate sessions with the parties, and may make suggestions and explore any ways of effecting a settlement. There will be no transcript or record of the proceedings at the meeting. The parties may either represent themselves or if they prefer appoint suitable persons to represent them. If any party will not be present at the meeting, one of the representatives must be given the authority by that party to agree a settlement of the dispute.

TERMINATION OF THE MEDIATION: The mediator may terminate the mediation at any time if he believes that the matters in dispute between the parties cannot be resolved by mediation. Any party to the mediation may withdraw prior to the meeting by writing to the mediator and all other parties to that effect, or by withdrawing from the meeting. At the conclusion of the mediation, whether resulting in settlement or not, the mediator will return all documents to the parties supplying them and destroy all his notes.

CONFIDENTIALITY: The mediation process, including administrative procedures, communication, meetings and private sessions with the mediator, is private and confidential, and no information arising from it shall be disclosed by the parties or the mediator to any non-party. Communication between the mediator and any party shall not be disclosed to the other party or parties without the agreement of the originating party. Furthermore, the mediation process is a *bona fide* attempt to resolve the dispute between the parties, and consequently the entire process is without prejudice. As such, all statements, documents and other information (whether oral or in writing) made in or arising out of the mediation shall not be discoverable or admissible in any legal, arbitration or other proceedings, save that any statement, document or other information which is otherwise discoverable or admissible shall not become non-admissible merely by virtue of its use in connection with the mediation. No party may call the mediator as a witness in any subsequent legal proceedings to give evidence concerning matters disclosed during the mediation.

EXCLUSION OF LIABILITY: The parties agree that the mediator shall not be liable in any way for any act or omission arising out of or in connection with the services provided by the mediator, his agents or servants, and such an undertaking shall be enforceable by the mediator.

COSTS: Each party shall bear its own costs of the mediation, and shall bear the costs of the mediation equally with the other party or parties.

SPECIAL NOTE: When the dispute arises out of a contract which incorporates a disputes procedure, the parties should agree how the timetable for settling the dispute should be altered to permit mediation. If any party has doubts, they should seek legal advice before taking any steps which might affect the contract dispute settlement procedure.

The contract being in the form of a deed is very useful. There is a perception amongst lay people that a deed is somehow more important than a simple written contract and the agreement being in this form has a salutary effect upon most parties.

THE IMPORTANCE OF THE CONTRACT

It can be seen that the contract embodies some very significant clause. Parties agree to share, in equal parts, the mediator's fees and disbursements. The mediator is vested with considerable autonomy as to how and where he should hold the meeting. It is also important to note that the parties have concurred with the fact that any party to the mediation may terminate it at any stage.

The authority of the parties

It is crucial to the procedure that at least one person on each side of the dispute has the absolute authority to make an agreement which otherwise would result in the inability of the parties to make any agreement and would thus be a complete waste of the parties' time and money and the mediator's time.

The confidentiality clause

The confidentiality clause is probably the most important as it encompasses the requirements for a mediation which includes the secrecy and the inability of the parties to use anything arising from the mediation in any later litigation. Also, they are barred from requiring the mediator to act as a witness in any later litigation.

In this respect it needs to be stated that the nature of mediation is such that, in a dispute, parts of it or the whole may be resolved. In the former case, the parties remain free to litigate on the issues which have not been settled but, by virtue of those issues which have been resolved, the court time required is much reduced and so is the cost of the action as a whole.

Agreement of costs

In a mediation it is possible and usual to resolve not only the various issues but to agree costs, making the procedure very attractive to both parties and their lawyers.

THE DIFFERENCE BETWEEN CONCILIATION AND MEDIATION

It is the ability to discuss issues confidentially between themselves without the discussions being capable of being used against them later that makes mediation such an attractive procedure to the parties and identifies it as totally different from conciliation, as defined in the process of medical complaints, which has no place in the field of litigation.

In making this comment, it should be noted that the term conciliation is frequently applied to processes which equate to the term mediation as used in this book. If the use of the term is synonymous with the term mediation, then the benefits ascribable to the process are identical to those attributable to mediation. The comments made are not intended to detract from the use made by those organisations such as the Institute of Chartered Engineers, whose conciliation scheme is eminently successful. This particular scheme is one of many regularly and successfully referred to in contracts and which have all been equally successful in resolving matters which would otherwise have inevitably resulted in prolonged litigation.

In the context of this book, the term conciliation is used only in respect of the attempt made in medical disciplinary procedures to bring the parties together, but which does not have the benefit of being a 'without prejudice' process. With conciliation, there is the possibility of the doctor becoming involved in a further disciplinary process if anything is said during the conciliation which reveals a potential disciplinary problem.

THE SUCCESS RATE OF MEDIATION

The success rate of mediation is impressive. Figures indicate that, once the idea has been put forward, and provided that it is transmitted to the other party by a neutral third party, the uptake rate is in the order of 70%. Once the mediation has been accepted as a concept by the parties, the rate of resolution of disputes is in the order of 90%. This rate is reflected almost universally by those who practice widely in the field.

Mediation in multi-party disputes

How does mediation work? The mediator, once appointed, will make contact, usually in writing with both (or indeed all) parties. There is absolutely no reason why mediation should not be used in multi-party disputes.

In the medical world, this means that where a dispute involves more than one doctor or separate entities such as a general practice and a hospital trust as well as a patient and/or their relatives, the process is of great use.

The preliminary contact

Once the mediator has made contact with the parties, he will probably decide that a meeting would be advantageous. However, in a not insignificant number of cases, the dispute may be resolved by the mediator telephoning or writing to the parties and helping them reach a satisfactory agreement.

The major advantage of mediation is that the parties can agree to ways of settling a dispute which would be impossible for a court or an arbitrator to decide upon.

EXAMPLES OF DISPUTES RESOLVED BY MEDIATION

Some examples of disputes, medical and non-medical may help the reader in understanding the way in which a mediation can assist in settling a matter.

1. The parties to the dispute were an Engineering Company (A) and a Firm (B) which produced goods. B ordered from A some heavy plant consisting of two major machines. The first was paid for but the second was not. There were allegations that the plant had not functioned adequately and that B's trade had been severely damaged. The mediator discovered that A was under some considerable financial pressure and desperately wanted payment for the second machine. B, on the other hand, also had severe financial difficulties not directly attributable to the machinery. They were, however, not in a position to pay the outstanding sums.

If the matter had come to court, it is certain that there would have been a claim and counterclaim, with much dispute over the facts. Financing the litigation would have been a horrendous burden. The outcome was uncertain, although it is almost certain that A would obtain judgment in respect of the cost of the machinery whilst B would less probably obtain judgment for some damages in respect of the failure of the machinery to function according to specification. What was certain is that if the matter went to trial both parties would end up in liquidation.

The mediator obtained an agreement that B would pay A the outstanding amounts over a period of several months with agreed dates for each payment. The first payment was made and then the second failed to materialise.

Mediation was again invoked and it was discovered that B was just about to go into involuntary liquidation. There being no hope of any further payments being made to A, the mediator arranged for title in the machinery to be returned to A, who gave up any rights to a further claim on B. B granted A a licence to enter his premises, dismantle and remove his machinery. Because of the proximity of B's landlord revoking the lease to the premises, he was approached and granted a further licence in the same terms.

A rapidly dismantled the machinery and recovered it. The machinery was protected from creditors of B. A managed to resell the machinery and stayed solvent. B sadly did not.

This case shows the way in which a solution can be reached which a court would find difficult to achieve and the way in which a party can be protected from difficulties that would otherwise arise. The solution was by no means perfect but one party, at least, was rescued and the way in which this was done was certainly equitable.

2. The personal injury dispute between a third party insurer and an individual devolved around quantum (the amount recoverable in damages). The insurer felt that his offer was adequate but the claimant thought otherwise. Mediation was invoked and the mediator ascertained that the insurer was willing to increase his offer by a relatively small amount. The total quantum was under £4,000. The final deficit was around £800. There being no compromise on either side, it looked as though the matter would proceed to a court judgment. The mediator suggested to the insurer that it might consider offering a year's free insurance to the claimant who, but for their insured, had a 21-year clean driving record. He added that the probability was that having recruited the claimant the insurer would keep the claimant as a customer and receive normal premiums in the future. The claimant agreed to the offer provided that his 'No Claims Bonus' was protected. This was agreed and the matter resolved. Both parties were pleased with the outcome and the cost of the exercise was a fraction of what it would have been had the matter proceeded along the traditional court route.

These two cases show dramatically how the use of mediation can resolve what may at first seem to be an insoluble problem. It requires a mediator who is capable of lateral thinking and who can suggest to the parties appropriate solutions.

3. A third history provides an insight into a group of disputes which constitute a headache to any claims manager.

The case involved a claim for a small sum, under £1,000, which the insurer would have liked to settle on commercial grounds, but he knew full well that by doing so he would face the potential for a large number of similar claims. Defending the case would probably result in a judgment for the insurer, but being such a small claim he would not recover costs. Any court case would also be associated with publicity which would, again, inevitably generate a string of new claims. Putting the case to a mediator, it was agreed that liability could be a problem, although not perhaps insuperable. The claimant was self-representing and had unreasonable expectations, all of which presaged badly for the insurer. A small settlement was agreed and the contract which was used to settle it contained a clause to the effect that the claimant would not publish the agreement and if they did they would pay back the sum granted by a multiple.

There is certainly some doubt as to the enforceability of such an agreement, but to date the author is not aware of any breaches of such terms.

4. Finally, a fourth case in which a claim was made against an insurer, in respect of the death of a party.

The estate was claiming a sum in excess of £600,000 and the insurer denied liability. At the ensuing mediation, liability was admitted but the insurer claimed that there was a significant element of contributory negligence. An offer of below £100,000 was made. The mediator helped the parties agree the contributory negligence and then addressed quantum and finally the case resolved for a sum in excess of the first offered by the insurer but considerably below the claim of the estate. Massive legal costs were saved, and the agreement was brought about by the highly competent legal advisers instructed by the estate and the sound judgment of the insurer.

THE WITHDRAWAL OF A CASE WITH NO MERIT

One result which is rarely if ever discussed under the heading of mediation is the ability of a good mediator to cause a plaintiff with no recognisable case to withdraw. It is a critical benefit of mediation that a case can be settled in these circumstances.

The emotional issues

In medical matters where there are issues of great emotional significance and probably issues which one or other party would not want openly discussed in public, the advantages cannot be overestimated.

Because of these highly charged emotional situations, a few cases have got to a stage of side issues such as actions for defamation and, through the mediation process, these can often be simply resolved by agreement to withdraw in return for agreement to refrain from further publishing the libel.

Justice to be done

One problem which may arise is the plaintiff's wish to 'see justice done', alternatively stated as being a wish for revenge, and possibly to see the defendant suffer. Whilst few will admit to this, the usual comment being 'I'm not doing it for money but to make sure it never happens to anyone else'. Off the record, the truth is more revealing being translated as 'I'll ... the ... for everything I can ... get'. This motive needs to be dealt with and it is through the offices of the mediator that this is possible.

THE MEETING

Prior to this meeting, the mediator may well have invited each party to prepare a summary of his case on a sheet of A4 paper and no more. This exercise has resulted in many mediations collapsing as the case immediately settles once those involved have been forced to concentrate on the actual issues.

The meeting which the mediator arranges is the chance for the claimant or plaintiff to 'have his day in court'. The mediator conducts his opening meeting in a formal manner. His opening address will consist of an introduction of both himself and a chance for each of the parties present to introduce himself. It is also the chance to confirm that one person in each party has the authority to settle the issues on behalf of himself or his party.

Following these introductory issues, the mediator will invite each party to address him and explain the issues. The importance of this address cannot be overestimated. The party is not acting as an advocate in a court by trying to appraise the mediator of all the facts of the claim or defence, the evidence and legal issues. Rather, the parties' address is a means of outlining the broad base of their position to help the mediator grasp the essential facts. More importantly, however, it represents the moment at which claimants can 'have their day in court'.

It is this address which provides the opportunity for the claimant or plaintiff to speak in a way that would not be possible for a lay client in a trial, and also to speak in a way that traditional legal wisdom would frown upon. Whatever is said, however, no damage to the position of the party can occur. Unlike an arbitration where it is critical that the arbitrator hears the evidence and only the evidence, a mediator has no need to be appraised of the finer details of the case since the purpose of the procedure is for the parties themselves to decide upon all matters, with the mediator serving to facilitate such decisions. Thus the time can be usefully used by giving the plaintiff his 'day in court'. Being on a 'without prejudice' basis, the lawyers have nothing to fear, and the mediator should by his presence prevent any violent outbursts which could give rise to further personal injury.

The importance of the mediator controlling this meeting should therefore not be underestimated.

After the introductory meeting

Following this meeting, the mediator will invite the parties to go to private rooms and it is from this point that constructive settlement discussions take place.

The mediator will discuss the case with each party in turn, attempting to find out what they really want and what they are prepared to forego.

Constructive consideration of position

Each party will be encouraged to consider their position and make constructive decisions as to ways in which the matter can be progressed.

Confidentiality guaranteed

These discussions are to be conducted in absolute confidence and nothing which is said within these private rooms will be transmitted by the mediator to any other party without the absolute authority of that party.

Avoiding misunderstandings

The party should write down any offer which they desire the mediator to transmit to another party. The alternative is for the mediator to write it down and have a representative of that party sign it.

In this way, the mediator is protected from allegations that he has breached confidence and it further imparts to the parties the positive nature of the confidentiality, thus enhancing the probability that those involved will discuss issues freely with the mediator.

Progress and offers

As the mediation progresses, various offers will be made to the other party(ies) as will counter offers. Eventually, in by far the greatest number of cases, a final resolution will evolve and final agreement will be made.

THE AGREEMENT

The question of enforceability of an agreement concluded under a mediation always arises and it is certainly important to understand some of the ways in which the agreement can be reduced to an enforceable agreement.

Form of the agreement

Although the negotiations are made on a 'without prejudice' basis, once the terms of the agreement have been agreed by all parties to the dispute they are *de facto* an enforceable agreement.

However, it must be borne in mind that the parties are already in dispute and the last thing the mediator wants is to produce an even more acrimonious dispute to replace the one he has resolved.

If, as is preferable, the parties have been assisted in resolving the dispute by the presence of lawyers, it is possible to use their services to draft the terms of agreement into a contract which the parties can sign and which will then be binding upon them.

If the matter is too complex to draft at the time, then heads of agreement can be drafted and signed, allowing for enforceability and for the legal advisers to draft the final contract at their leisure.

Enforceability of the agreement

In some matters the parties may be completely unable to trust the other party to comply and in these circumstances the parties may agree to appoint the mediator as an arbitrator to deliver a consent award.

This technique has a number of advantages for all parties. Firstly, the resulting award, which would be deemed to have been made under the auspices of s 51 of the Arbitration Act 1996, is enforceable through the courts on the basis of it being an arbitral award (see s 66 of the Arbitration Act 1996).

It is possible that some argument could be raised as to whether or not there was an actual arbitration if the Arbitrator was not properly appointed and a degree of care should be taken in the appointment to avoid it being open to criticism.

This means that the arbitrator should be appointed to resolve the dispute but should then be provided with the consent agreement to settle, which he can then convert to an award.

CHAPTER EIGHT

MEDARB

Medarb is a hybrid between arbitration and mediation and is generally less well understood by lawyers than mediation. It is liable to engender a wide range of responses from those who know little about it.

Medarb combines the benefits of mediation with the certainty of arbitration.

The most lucid explanation of the procedure can be obtained from a specimen Medarb contract which is reproduced below.

SPECIMEN AGREEMENT TO MEDARB

AGREEMENT TO MEDIATION/ARBITRATION

1. The following disputes have arisen between the parties.
2. The disputants have agreed to request the mediator to accept the appointment as mediator for the settlement of these disputes.
3. The disputants have agreed that the mediator should conduct the mediation in accordance with the attached guidelines.

This DEED is made on   between the disputants and the mediator both named below.

IT IS AGREED

1. The mediator accepts the appointment and agrees to conduct the mediation in accordance with the attached guidelines for mediation.
2. The disputants hereby agree that should any disputant notify the mediator that he wishes to terminate the mediation or that the mediator should decide that a resolution is unlikely, then the said disputant or the mediator, as appropriate, shall give notice to the other disputants and the mediator, if appropriate, that the mediation be concluded, and upon receipt of such notice the mediator shall thereby be appointed arbitrator to resolve matters in accordance with the Arbitration Act 1996.

An alternative clause 2 is:

The disputants hereby agree that should any disputant notify the mediator that he wishes to terminate the mediation or the mediator should decide that a resolution is unlikely, then the said disputant or the mediator, as appropriate, shall give notice to the other disputants and the mediator, if appropriate, that the mediation be concluded, and that upon receipt of such notice the mediator shall notify all parties of the fact that the mediation has failed. The mediator shall as soon thereafter as is practicable appoint an arbitrator to resolve the dispute in accordance with the Arbitration Act 1996. The parties agree that any such person appointed by the mediator will be accepted by them as arbitrator and that he or she shall be deemed by them to be appointed by them, in writing under the terms of the aforementioned Arbitration Act.

3. The disputants bind themselves jointly and severally to pay upon demand the mediator's fees and disbursements in accordance with the rates set out in the attached Schedule. The disputants between themselves settle all costs of the mediation in accordance with the guidelines.

4. The disputants agree that they will jointly and severally indemnify the mediator against all claims demands proceedings damages costs charges and expenses which may arise in connection with or arising out of the mediation, or the way in which it is conducted and will not themselves bring any such claim against either of them.

SIGNED AS A DEED AND WITNESSED

First Disputant

(Name)

(Signature)

(Address)

(Date)

IN THE PRESENCE OF:

(Name)

(Address)

Second Disputant

(Name)

(Signature)

(Address)

(Date)

IN THE PRESENCE OF:

(Name)

(Address)

Third Disputant

(Name)

(Signature)

(Address)

(Date)

IN THE PRESENCE OF:

(Name)

(Address)

Fourth Disputant

(Name)

(Signature)

(Address)

(Date)

IN THE PRESENCE OF:

(Name)

(Address)

(Name)

Mediator

IN THE PRESENCE OF:

(Name)

(Address)

AGREEMENT TO MEDIATE APPLICATION No:

SCHEDULE TO THE AGREEMENT TO MEDIATION

THE MEDIATOR'S FEE: The mediator will be paid at the rate of £   per hour with a minimum fee of £   . Time spent by the mediator in travelling will be charged at   % of the hourly fee.

DISBURSEMENTS: The mediator will charge at cost any disbursements properly made in respect of:

(a) Telephone calls, faxes and other forms of communication.

(b) Postage and any delivery charges.

(c) Travelling, hotel expenses, and similar expenses.

(d) Accommodation and other expenses relating to the venue for the mediation session.

(e) Mileage will be charged at per mile.

(f) Any taxes such as VAT which are required to be charged by law will be added to the above charges as is appropriate.

The mediator will be entitled to receive payment for disbursements, in advance of incurring them, from any party. The party who pays any such sum to the mediator will be able to recover an equal share of such payment from the other parties to the dispute as a debt due.

SPECIAL TERMS

GUIDELINES TO MEDIATION INTRODUCTION

Mediation is a process whereby a dispute between two or more persons or companies is resolved by remitting the dispute to a private hearing before an independent neutral third party (the mediator) whose role is to assist the parties to reach a mutually satisfactory solution to the matters in dispute. The mediator may not impose a settlement on the parties.

THE MEDIATOR: Unless specified otherwise, the term the mediator, within the context of these guidelines shall be read as   (name of mediator).

USE OF THE GUIDELINES: Unless otherwise specified by the parties, these guidelines shall be deemed to be part of the parties' agreement to mediate, although the parties may by agreement vary these guidelines.

CONFIRMATION OF MEDIATOR: The mediator shall not embark upon the mediation without the written approval of the parties to the dispute which is to be mediated. Before such approval is given, the mediator shall disclose to the parties any interest he may have in the dispute or with any of the parties, and any other circumstances likely to affect the presumption of impartiality.

MEETING OF THE PARTIES WITH THE MEDIATOR: As soon as is practicable (and in any event within two weeks) after his appointment, the mediator will arrange a meeting before him of all the parties to the dispute. The mediator will fix the date, time, and venue of the meeting. The mediator may request further details of the facts or issues from the parties. At least seven days before the meeting, each party to the dispute may provide the mediator with a brief memorandum setting out the relevant facts and issues in the dispute, and their position on these issues. The mediator may send the memorandum to the other parties. Prior to the meeting, the parties should not forward any other documents to the mediator, unless at his specific request. If necessary, the mediator may, with the agreement of the parties, visit any place relevant to the dispute, or seek legal or other advice. On any visit, the mediator should be accompanied by a representative of all the parties.

CONDUCT OF THE MEETING: The parties should bring to the meeting all documents and information which they may wish to bring to the attention of the mediator. At the meeting, the mediator may hold joint or separate sessions with the parties, and may make suggestions and explore any ways of effecting a settlement. There will be no transcript or record of the proceedings at the meeting. The parties may either represent themselves or if they prefer appoint suitable persons to represent them. If any party will not be present at the meeting, one of the representatives must be given the authority by that party to agree a settlement of the dispute.

TERMINATION OF THE MEDIATION: The mediator may terminate the mediation at any time if he believes that the matters in dispute between the parties cannot be resolved by mediation. Any party to the mediation may withdraw prior to the meeting by writing to the mediator and all other parties to that effect, or by withdrawing from the meeting. At the conclusion of the mediation, whether resulting in settlement or not, the mediator will return all documents to the parties supplying them and destroy all his notes.

CONFIDENTIALITY: The mediation process, including administrative procedures, communication, meetings and private sessions with the mediator, is private and confidential, and no information arising from it shall be disclosed by the parties or the mediator to any non-party. Communication between the mediator and any party shall not be disclosed to the other party or parties without the agreement of the originating party. Furthermore, the mediation process is a *bona fide* attempt to resolve the dispute between the parties, and consequently the entire process is without prejudice. As such, all statements, documents and other information (whether oral or in writing) made in or arising out of the mediation shall not be discoverable or admissible in any legal, arbitration or other proceedings, save that any statement, document or other information which is otherwise discoverable or admissible shall not become non-admissible merely by virtue of its use in connection with the mediation. No party may call the mediator as a witness in any subsequent legal proceedings to give evidence concerning matters disclosed during the mediation.

EXCLUSION OF LIABILITY: The parties agree that the mediator shall not be liable in any way for any act or omission arising out of or in connection with the services provided by the mediator, his agents or servants, and such an undertaking shall be enforceable by the mediator.

COSTS: Each party shall bear its own costs of the mediation, and shall bear the costs of the mediation equally with the other party or parties.

SPECIAL NOTE: When the dispute arises out of a contract which incorporates a disputes procedure, the parties should agree how the timetable for settling the dispute should be altered to permit mediation. If any party has doubts, they should seek legal advice before taking any steps which might affect the contract dispute settlement procedure.

THE MEDIATOR AS ARBITRATOR

It can be seen from the above contract that the parties agree as with the earlier example to submit the dispute to mediation but they then go further in agreeing that if the matter is not resolved by this process they will appoint the mediator as an arbitrator to resolve the matter by arbitration.

Difficulties associated with appointing mediator as arbitrator

There are certain problems which can arise from this; not the least is the fact that the mediator will have been privy to some of the 'without prejudice' negotiations and it takes a very strong willed person to cast such knowledge out of his mind.

Desirability of appointing mediator as arbitrator

Despite this handicap, if this is what the parties desire, it is a most effective method of resolving the dispute. Further, as the mediator has some deep knowledge of the matters in dispute, it will be less onerous for the parties to ensure that he is fully appraised of the relevant facts.

Importance of securing status of arbitrator

If such a transition is contemplated, the parties should be invited to 'reappoint' him in writing at the time that the decision to proceed down that avenue is made.

This action ensures that neither party can later claim that the appointment was made prior to a realisation of the implications, which has the effect of reducing the chances of a court ruling that the arbitrator should be removed.

An alternative to appointing the mediator as arbitrator

If the parties consider that it would be detrimental to appoint the mediator as an arbitrator then the alternative clause 2 (incorporated in the specimen agreement above) overcomes this difficulty and yet allows the parties the certainty which they desire.

Does this contract resolve disputes more readily

Experience has shown that the difficulties noted above very often result in the parties resolving the matter by mediation. This means that both the parties and the mediator have a preference for the first method of appointing an arbitrator which, despite the possibility of difficulties, is associated with considerable cost savings and appears to be acceptable to all.

It can thus be seen that the relatively draconian and possibly legally problematical contract can, by the very nature of its existence, lead the parties to resolve a matter in a manner which would probably not have been possible without the overt threat of an arbitrated decision.

CHAPTER NINE

COMPLAINTS

Complaints against doctors and other medical staff have reached epidemic proportions. The effect on morale and thus the service delivered is of massive significance. Anything which can be done to reduce the stress on the professions and which can increase the faith of the complainant in the means used to deal with the complaint must be of the greatest benefit.

INTRODUCTORY REMARKS

This chapter is devoted to complaints against doctors and others who front the medical services of this country. It does not pretend to address all the ways in which complaints are or can be dealt with, and specifically does not address the statutory complaints procedures.

It is felt that those involved in complaints could benefit from having an alternative and totally independent means of dealing with complaints; a method which, hopefully, the complainant would also see as being independent.

The financial cost of dealing with complainants is escalating, the morale of those complained about is sinking and the faith of those making complaints is at rock bottom in respect of the available procedures.

THE CAUSE OF COMPLAINTS

The above paragraph outlines the sorry state of the medical world, beset by financial restraint and managed by those who now have to consider the commercial means of reducing costs. This may mean that a complaint is admitted because the cost of investigating it would be too great. This results in those being complained about feeling, justifiably, that they are being made scapegoats and the effect on morale is monumental.

Managers seem, to those making complaints, to be too protective and they are generally not trusted by complainants to carry out unbiased investigations. This leads to increased litigation since it is perceived to be the only way to get a proper investigation of the matter.

THE OUTCOME OF COMPLAINTS

Whilst the majority of complaints are successfully handled by those charged with doing so, not all are. Local investigation may fail to resolve only a few but these are important to all the parties concerned. Liability may be accepted but quantum (the amount recoverable in damages) might be too low for the plaintiff to obtain Legal Aid. If the case is pursued through the courts, the possibility of a plaintiff in person arises which in most cases leads to poor conduct of the case and high costs. If the plaintiff chooses to pursue the case, the cost will probably be a multiple of quantum and the defence will almost certainly not recover the major part of their expenditure in any circumstances.

A NOVEL SCHEME FOR DEFUSING THE DIFFICULT COMPLAINT

It is suggested that the scheme outlined below could beneficially be applied to complaints that fall within the parameters described above. It provides an 'open investigation' in a closed environment, and it allows the complainant to feel he has been heard. This defuses most complaints, particularly if an apology is obtained, where appropriate. The whole proceedings are managed on a 'without prejudice' basis. This ensures that nothing arising could be used if the matter should proceed to litigation, a most unlikely event. It is also possible to build in a confidentiality clause (see above under 'Mediation').

An important aspect of the scheme is for the authority to ensure that the complainant is represented legally. This serves two purposes. The first is that it provides the complainant with the feeling that his interests are being protected, a fact which is undoubtedly correct. The second aspect is that his position is again protected in the event that an agreement is drafted and signed. It cannot be said at a later stage that the agreement was obtained improperly or under duress. This again provides the authority with the certainty that they need.

The scheme outlined below is a skeleton argument for a system which can be invoked in the case that the in-house complaints procedures have failed to produce a resolution and where there is at least the possibility of litigation.

The experience of many health authorities is that certain departments, especially those in the forefront such as accident and emergency departments, are being faced with a much greater number of complaints than before patients' charters and other such encouragements to complain about the professions were promulgated.

The very nature of the complaints is such that it is now far from certain that litigation will not follow in some cases and indeed many administrators report that in-house complainants services appear to be fishing trips for potential litigants.

The above comments do not ignore the fact that the great majority of complainants are properly and expeditiously dealt with through in-house procedures.

This scheme is meant to deal with the 'complaint which will not go away' and which, although it possibly involves a negligence claim, is one where quantum is likely to be small.

Despite the fact that quantum may be low, such claims are not without their effect on the morale of those working in the department and furthermore, the legal expense bill may be totally disproportionate to the level of the claim.

The existence of Legal Aid means that some complainants can pursue what are almost hopeless cases and, even if they lose, the authority is unable to recover costs.

Further, the present move to restrict Legal Aid means that there are more unrepresented plaintiffs and although the claim has little or no merit plaintiffs will pursue it without sound legal advice. The inevitable cost to the authority and its staff is high.

The skeleton outline of a scheme is shown here as an aid to helping the reader consider what is, in effect, a revolutionary departure from present practice.

THE SCENARIO

A patient has made a complaint which has arisen from a real or perceived 'injustice'. The complaint may be accompanied by a claim for damages, but in any event, even if proved, the loss would be small, say under £5,000. Lawyers may or may not have been instructed to act for the 'plaintiff'.

The proposition

It is proposed that a 'without prejudice' meeting is arranged by an 'outside agency'. The complainant or plaintiff, hereafter referred to as the complainant, is invited to attend with, if appropriate, their legal adviser.

The health authority is represented by the consultant in charge of the department under criticism or the consultant in charge of the complainant's medical care. Also present should be the doctor or staff member against whom the complaint is directed, and the trust's legal adviser.

The meeting should aim to give the complainant a chance to voice their complaint and for the 'individual' to answer. This should be done under the controlling influence of the 'mediator'.

If it is concluded that there was a fault on the part of the authority or its staff, the second stage should be to settle the claim.

In this way, legal costs are significantly reduced, the trust is not making unreasonable concessions, paying out only where it believes it should.

Most complaints should resolve entirely under these circumstances.

COSTING

The trust will pay for the process but if several cases are dealt with at the same time, the cost per case is infinitesimal. This can be set against future legal costs which have been avoided.

The trust should also agree to make a fixed fee contribution towards the plaintiff or complainant if so requested, as Legal Aid will not contribute to this procedure. A figure of £100 might well be equitable.

THE DEPARTMENT OF HEALTH'S PILOT MEDIATION SCHEME

The Department of Health have currently been involved in a trial of mediation as a means of resolving medical negligence disputes. It will be some time before the results of the trial are available but recent hearsay is to the effect that it has not so far found favour with the health authority advisers involved in the mediations so far undertaken.

The reasons for any failure will of course be discussed during the public *post mortem*. The schemes outlined and discussed in this book do not however, resemble anything that has been put forward by the Department and, in both its use and scope, it has no similarities.

The reader will fully appreciate the type of case which it is envisaged might be helped by this scheme and hopefully those charged with dealing with such matters will feel able to break away from the traditional mould.

CHAPTER TEN

CONCILIATION

The term 'conciliation' as used in medical complaints procedures is the current 'in thing', the 'buzz word' of those who purport to be socially correct. It is not, and never will be, a subject which has any role to play in a book on legal proceedings except to ensure that it is excluded from consideration.

INTRODUCTION

The terms of reference used in discussing conciliation are those which apply to the process which is currently utilised under the auspices of the NHS of the United Kingdom, and not to the various schemes used within a number of commercial contracts which conform to the requirements of the process described under the heading in this book of 'Mediation'.

Conciliation and mediation are frequently interchanged in general usage but the use made of the words in this chapter are entirely specific.

CONCILIATION IN THE NATIONAL HEALTH SERVICE

Over the last few years, along with patient charters and other political decrees, conciliation has blossomed. Family practitioner committees, then family health service authorities and now health authorities, have encouraged general practitioners to submit complaints against them to conciliation. Armies of enthusiastic, half-trained lay personnel try to make good in circumstances where wiser persons would fear to tread.

None of this is to detract from some of the exceedingly competent persons who have successfully defused complaints and restored the patient to his doctor. However, conciliation is not without its problems and it is these problems which make it such a dangerous and unacceptable process in the majority of cases.

THE REGULATION OF THE NHS SCHEME

In *Practice Based Complaints Procedures Guidance for General Practices*, 1996 (NHS Executive), the following text is relevant:

> **7.9** As noted above, a major feature of the new procedures is the separation of complaints and disciplinary procedures – there will be no direct connection between complaints procedures and disciplinary action. But it is possible that some complaints will reveal information about serious matters which indicate a possible need for disciplinary investigation.
>
> Where it proves necessary, disciplinary action will continue to be linked to the terms of service and will therefore apply only to medical practitioners included in a health authority list. If there appears to be a need for a disciplinary investigation, your health authority will consider whether informal action might be helpful before invoking disciplinary procedures. For example, the authority might suggest to the doctor that he or she undergoes training in a specific area or finds help to improve practice procedures.

Although not reproduced para 6.3 is relevant as it involves authority staff in complaints and refers to conciliation, the indication being that health authority staff may become involved in it.

THE RELATIONSHIP OF THE DOCTOR, PATIENT AND HEALTH AUTHORITY

One problem in the NHS is that the patient has no contractual relationship with the doctor, who is a subcontractor to the health authority. There are very few practitioners who are direct employees of the health authority and so they are disregarded for the purposes of this paragraph.

Conciliation has been around for a long time and in the Institute of Chartered Engineers contract, the parties are committed to conciliation in the event of a dispute. The conciliation is undertaken and, if no satisfactory resolution is made, a recommendation is made by the conciliator which is binding upon the parties unless they choose to appeal.

This differs from the NHS scheme which has no such certainty and, more important, is the fact that it is a part of a disciplinary procedure, albeit a 'semi voluntary' one. The essence of a successful mediation or conciliation is that the parties to it participate as a voluntary act.

This is therefore, a feature which it is difficult to instil into the NHS system.

IN-HOUSE COMPLAINTS PROCEDURES

There has been a move in the NHS to encourage the use of in-house complaints procedures. This is a move which should be treated with caution although it will, if handled sympathetically, result in a reduction of matters reaching the authority as complaints. The present system, however, does not provide either an impartial hearing or complete independence, and thus it suffers from all the problems highlighted in this chapter. It is not possible to have an employee of a practice, particularly one in a lower position than the principals, perceived as being independent of either party and thus the probability is that patients will fail to view this procedure in the light of a true conciliation, although if the conciliator is particularly skilled and personable they might achieve a resolution.

THE CONCEPT OF CONCILIATION

The concept of conciliation is that of a third party coming between the parties to a dispute, helping them to understand the other party's view and agree a resolution and, if necessary, admit a fault.

THE DIFFICULTIES OF CONCILIATION

The potential difficulties which arise from this procedure are legion.

First, the current systems are not uniformly funded independently of the parties and this must necessarily cast doubt on the credibility of the system.

As previously mentioned, the quality of conciliators is, to say the least, variable and experience has shown that a significant number try to work by holding a meeting and then try to prevent the parties arguing. This has the instant effect of inflaming what is already a contentious situation and the result is that, far from resolving the problem, a deeper and more intractable one can evolve.

Perhaps the most dangerous aspect of the whole process is that it does not have the formal status of a 'without prejudice' procedure and thus it can be used by the complainant as a means to determine the strengths and weaknesses of their case.

The fact that there is no recognition of the 'without prejudice' basis, means that the only way in which the position of the practitioner being complained about can be protected is by a three-way contractual obligation to observe confidence of the proceedings. The level of protection this would provide if litigation should evolve is dubious. The contract would need to include the conciliator.

Can conciliation be recommended in complaints

The inevitable conclusion is that conciliation is too fraught with hazard to be contemplated by any party who is potentially a defendant in the course of litigation or arbitration proceedings.

The only sensible advice one could give to a medical practitioner faced with a potential legal problem arising in the course of his professional duties would be to say that conciliation has no place in the resolution of such a dispute but, if he chooses to submit the matter to conciliation, he clearly runs the risk of anything arising from the conciliation being used against him at a later stage.

The future for conciliation in complaints

If conciliation is to become a truly useful and recognised concept within the NHS, then a number of features will need to change. The most difficult concept to overcome will be the fact that it is a part of a potential disciplinary procedure and until this changes it is difficult to see how it can be acceptable in the face of the difficulties outlined above.

If it is to become accepted, and the problems associated with it being a disciplinary issue are to be overcome, there must be a number of changes to the system, amongst these must be the following.

The process must be recognised as being a 'without prejudice' process and the Regulations must incorporate this.

There is good precedent for this in the Employment Protection (Consolidation) Act 1978 and ss 133 and 134 of this Act provide that evidence given to conciliation officers will not be admissible in evidence in any later proceedings.

The present system runs at least the risk that information gathered by a conciliator could be used by the authority in any later disciplinary action or, worse, could result in the commencement of such action. Until this is overcome, conciliation can have no place in the resolution of complaints.

WHO CAN CONCILIATE

The personnel must be fully and properly trained and able to understand the ramifications of any discussions which arise during a conciliation. This should not be interpreted to mean that lawyers should be the conciliators. Their training is essentially adversarial and not necessarily a suitable background for such a post.

FUNDING CONCILIATION

It is crucial that the personnel are adequately paid and the salary should be commensurate with the position and responsibilities. What level is appropriate is always difficult to determine but, in view of the implications of their involvement, a suggested figure would be an hourly rate in the region of parity with a middle grade solicitor in private practice.

In so far as the NHS is concerned, funding must be such that none of the parties to the conciliation are obliged to pay for the services of the conciliator. This means that funding will need to be central to the point of use.

The risk of not charging the complainant

If there is no financial commitment on the part of a party, particularly the complainant, there is an immediate incentive to make trivial and ultimately unsustainable complaints. The system should therefore, ideally, allow for a costs implication in the event of the complaint being trivial and vexatious. This, however, would lead to a need to decide which complaints were vexatious and also to nominate someone to make the decision. The fact that the decision may later need to be enforced and that a suitable appeals procedure needs to be in place suggest that this topic should be left well alone.

If the parties are a general practitioner and a patient, the level of funding should be at or above the District Health Authority.

Who should employ the conciliator

The status of the conciliator needs to be considered. They should be adequately trained and there is a powerful argument for making them full-time employees of an authority. However, if they are to be effective in resolving the dispute they need to be able to instil confidence in the parties. The fact that they are employees of a health authority would almost certainly result in a practitioner feeling vulnerable to 'opening up in discussions', and might well make a complainant doubt the independence of the procedure.

THE IDEA OF A NEW QUANGO

Perhaps the most acceptable course of action for the state health service is for it to have an independent body, funded centrally, and able to supply professionally competent conciliators to any authority within the service. The financial arrangements between the conciliator and the agency would be of no concern to the health authority or its staff. The conciliator would report administratively to the unit and there would be a statutory provision that the conciliator would provide no information to anyone but the parties, with the exception of administrative details as to the time and place of a conciliation and the names of the parties, together with a report as to whether or not the conciliation was successful. The laws concerning child abuse and similar legislation would of course be complied with.

By working in this manner the standard of conciliators could be monitored and the way in which they would be paid should prevent the local authority seeking information to which they should not be entitled. This would also mean that there would be less detail to discover if the matter proceeded to litigation.

CONCLUSION

Having made these suggestions, the author accepts that it is totally improbable that any government would be likely to fund such a scheme and thus the advice that conciliation should be avoided must remain the best option for the majority of doctors.

CHAPTER ELEVEN

HOW TO CHOOSE THE CORRECT METHOD

Having decided that there is a dispute, the next decision is how to resolve it. This chapter provides some help in making that decision.

THE DISPUTE HAS ARISEN

The party who believes he has been harmed will, more often than not, seek help from a lawyer. Thus he, at least in the first instance, will be committed to litigation.

The lawyer

After seeking appropriate documentation and other evidence, the solicitor will be in a position to advise his client as to whether or not there is a reasonable chance of success in pursuing the case.

The contract

At this stage it may become apparent to the party that he has a contractual duty to consider alternative methods of pursuing the case, such as arbitration, or he may find that he is obliged to attempt to mediate the dispute at first instance.

If his contract is one such as that promulgated by the ICE, his choice will have been made for him and the conciliation clause to which he has subscribed will all but resolve the dispute for him.

Although drifting away from the field of medical disputes, many contracts contain a binding arbitration clause which commits both parties to the dispute to submit it to an arbitrator, normally one appointed by a specified body or person.

THE STAY OF PROCEEDINGS

In this respect even if a party has commenced litigation, in the presence of such an agreement, the court will upon application stay proceedings to allow the arbitration to continue. This particular aspect is covered by s 9 Arbitration Act 1996.

Section 9 Arbitration Act 1996

9 – (1) A party to an arbitration agreement against whom legal proceedings are brought (whether by way of claim or counterclaim) in respect of a matter which under the agreement is to be referred to arbitration may (upon notice to the other parties to the proceedings) apply to the court in which the proceedings have been brought to stay the proceedings so far as that matter.

(2) An application may be made notwithstanding that the matter is to be referred to arbitration only after the exhaustion of other dispute resolution procedures.

(3) An application may not be made by a person before taking the appropriate procedural step (if any) to acknowledge the legal proceedings against him or after he has taken any step in those proceedings to answer the substantive claim.

(4) On application under this section the court shall grant a stay unless satisfied that the arbitration agreement is null and void, inoperative, or incapable of being performed.

(5) If the court refuses to stay the legal proceedings, any provision that an award is a condition precedent to the bringing of legal proceedings in respect of any matter is of no effect in relation to those proceedings.

Reasons why the action may not be stayed

It is important for the parties to such an arbitration agreement to be aware that the court will, nearly always, and in most cases, regardless of the financial state of the parties, order that if the agreement is held valid then the litigation will be stayed. Although this is a somewhat simplified statement of the circumstances surrounding such an application, it is nevertheless a reasonable indication of the likely outcome. A prominent reason which might result in the court refusing to stay proceedings is the situation where the defendant is facing an allegation of fraud.

The plaintiff's financial situation is one factor which the courts will not usually take into account in deciding an application. This is demonstrated in the case of *Smith v Pearl Assurance Co Ltd* (1939). This might come as surprise since a party may be in a position to finance litigation through Legal Aid but not in a position to finance arbitration for which Legal Aid cannot be granted. This is a topic which is subject to discussion at the present time and there may eventually be a change in the way in which Legal Aid is granted.

In *Fakes v Taylor Woodrow Construction Co Ltd* (1973), an application was granted to the plaintiff who had commenced litigation whilst the defendants applied for the matter to be heard by an arbitrator. The issues were complex and involved monies owed by the defendant to the plaintiff which were substantial and the cause of his poverty.

Thus whilst the general position is that a stay will not be granted, the courts have an inherent right to allow the commencement of litigation if it is thought to be equitable.

So the choice as to whether the matter should be dealt with through the courts or through arbitration is relatively simple and, once it has been made, the appropriate form of action can be commenced.

Having made this decision the next matter to consider is whether or not it would be appropriate to commence mediation.

Should mediation be considered

The reader will recall that mediation can be commenced at any stage in the dispute from the moment a dispute arises to the moment before the judge or arbitrator decides the case.

In many ways, it is far better to consider mediation sooner rather than later. If one is going to mediate the dispute it is necessary that both parties have a firm idea of the issues, even if these 'boil down' to just one. As soon as the issues are appreciated it becomes possible to try to resolve them.

When to mediate

It is certainly not necessary to wait until the pleadings are closed or all expert and other witness statements have been exchanged. This said, in a matter of some complexity, it might well be appropriate to wait until this stage.

HOW TO GET THE OTHER PARTY TO THE TABLE

The party who is suggesting the idea of mediation might well find that the other party is reluctant to agree to the idea. This is not uncommon in adversarial proceedings where each party views the other with a substantial degree of suspicion.

Not infrequently, it has been found that if the idea is suggested by an independent company, rather than by the advocate for the party, success is more likely. There will be less suspicion and, in any event, the company personnel are far more likely to be able to 'sell the idea' since they are also more knowledgeable of the process.

Experience shows that if a letter is sent by the company to the party or their lawyer and is then followed up by a telephone call from a member of staff, the take-up rate for mediation is well in excess of 75%.

If the approach comes from the lawyers of one of the parties to the lawyers on the other side, the refusal rate is often in excess of 75%.

It can thus be seen that the company, as an independent broker, offers much to the process and allows each party to avoid being seen as 'pushy' or accepting.

CHAPTER TWELVE

FOREIGN JURISDICTIONS

There are many countries in the world and most have arbitration laws governing both domestic and international arbitrations. The importance of arbitration is such that the UN have promulgated a model law. Mediation also has a place in disputes, worldwide, although the importance and formality of mediation differs from country to country.

GENERAL COMMENTS

Arbitration and mediation are not the sole province of the English.

Arbitration is widely used throughout the world, particularly in the fields of commerce.

INTERNATIONAL RULES

The importance of the procedure can be judged from the fact that the United Nations Commission on International Trade Law has published two sets of draft rules.

The first, the UNCITRAL Arbitration Rules is a draft set of rules which of themselves are capable of providing a complete set of rules for the arbitration. These rules are reproduced in Appendix One of this book.

It will be noted that the rules can be modified by the parties, and the right to modify them is incorporated in the first clause.

The UNCITRAL model law is reproduced in Appendix Two of this book and represents an attempt to produce uniformity in the world's laws governing arbitration.

Whilst there has been no complete international adoption of the rules, there has been considerable adherence to them, in so far as individual countries are concerned.

The current Arbitration Act 1996, effective from 1 January 1997, owes much to the model law.

The importance of conformity in international arbitration law is probably the major reason for the inception of the model law.

In addition to the UNCITRAL Rules there are a very considerable number of other rules in existence. Some of them are mentioned here by title. For further information the bodies themselves should be contacted.

International Centre for Settlement of Investment Disputes

ICC Rules of Conciliation and Arbitration (ICC Publishing Paris)

The International Bar Rules of Evidence

Rules of Procedure of the Inter-American Commercial Arbitration Commission

Commercial Arbitration Rules of the American Arbitration Association

London Court of International Arbitration Rules

London Marine Arbitrators Association Terms

London Marine Arbitrators Association Small Claims Procedure

Grain And Feed Trade Association Arbitration Rules

Chartered Institute of Arbitrators Rules

Chartered Institute of Arbitrators Short Form Arbitration Rules

Sydney Maritime Arbitration Rules

The Charted Institute of Arbitrators also runs a number of schemes for organisations such as the Association of British Travel Agents, the Chartered Surveyors and a consumer arbitration scheme for FIMBRA.

SCOTLAND

Scotland is a separate jurisdiction from that of England and Wales and has a completely separate set of legislation under which arbitration is conducted. Despite this, however, arbitration is much used in Scotland and its arbitration laws are close to those of England and Wales.

NORTHERN IRELAND

Like Scotland, a separate jurisdiction from England and Wales exists but, again, the arbitration laws are similar to those of England and Wales.

In neither Scotland nor Northern Ireland is arbitration used in the resolution of medical negligence or personal injury.

This is due to the reluctance of the major defence bodies to contemplate arbitration as a means of dealing with cases of medical negligence. Until those who fund the bodies are perceived by those who run them as wanting to change the system, little significant change can be anticipated in this direction.

THE CHANNEL ISLANDS

The Channel Islands are a totally different jurisdiction from the rest of the United Kingdom and their legal system is founded on completely different principles.

Guernsey, which differs from Jersey, has a base of codified pre-Napoleonic French law with a strong admixture of English common law. Since the turn of the century the tendency has been to follow English common law more closely.

Because both islands have a high profile in the international financial markets, they are no novices to the advent of Alternative Dispute Resolution and indeed, in terms of arbitration, are considerably in advance of the rest of the United Kingdom where commercial matters are concerned.

Guernsey's arbitration law is contained in the Order in Council Projet de Loi The Arbitration (Guernsey) Law 1982, and the Arbitration (Amendment) (Guernsey) Law 1986.

In addition to these, a number of other orders and regulations apply covering such matters as evidence and procedure.

Many of the clauses of this law mirror the Arbitration Acts 1950 and 1979 passed by Parliament.

As with most other jurisdictions the award is enforceable by leave of the court (s 26) of the law.

EIRE

In Eire the use of mediation is hardly recognised. Within the last few years there has been a minor move towards the use of mediation in marital disputes but apart from this hardly any recognition has been given to the process. In the view of a solicitor in the jurisdiction, 'if two parties wished to discuss a legal dispute they would do so through their solicitor.' He continued by saying, 'In general, I think it should be borne in mind that Irish people like their day out in court. Certainly the legal profession does.'

Arbitration is recognised and has been legislated with the current Acts being the Arbitration Acts 1954 and 1980.

It is of interest that personal injury matters have only just been considered for arbitration and experience within the jurisdiction is that awards from arbitral tribunals in personal injury cases has been considerably in excess of the level of award which would be expected in a court.

Much of the experience has been derived from the Hepatitis B tribunals, from which substantial awards have been derived.

The awards do not always give certainty and, not infrequently, the terms of appointment of the arbitrator require that if a party is not satisfied with the award their right to litigate remains.

In commercial matters the use of arbitration is growing. In a recent case it was argued that an arbitration clause was an unfair contract term imposed on a consumer. The decision of the court was that it was not unfair and the court upheld the term.

All this means that the use of arbitration in Eire is limited for a number of very sound reasons.

A COMMENT ON HONG KONG

Hong Kong has a highly developed system of both arbitration and mediation. Both are actively promulgated in the jurisdiction and it is of notable effect that as early as the mid-eighties, the Hong Kong Institute of Engineers produced a clause in contracts for use by its members which was the catalyst for the process.

Well before this time, the legislators introduced the Arbitration Ordinance, Chapter 341 (Revised October 1990). As a leader in the commercial world it was felt necessary to ensure that the legislative framework to support arbitration should be in place. Currently, there are two separate sets of legislation in Hong Kong. The first, governing domestic arbitrations, is the legislation which incorporates much of the English Arbitration Acts 1950–79.

International arbitrations are governed by the UNCITRAL model law, with the references to the word 'commercial' having been deleted.

The Hong Kong International Arbitration Centre has had a very strong and beneficial influence upon the progress of arbitration in the country.

If invited to make a single comment upon the rules that govern arbitration in Hong Kong, the author would highlight r 32 which states that:

> Any party may avail himself of the procedure for a payment into court pursuant to Order 73 of the Rules of the Supreme Court of Hong Kong. No account shall be taken by the arbitrator of any written or oral offers of settlement where a payment into court could have been made.

This seemingly simple rule, if available in England, would overcome a sphere of difficulty which has been present for years and which will probably be present for many years to come. The current proposals by Lord Woolf may overcome this particular disability.

MEDIATION AND ARBITRATION IN THE UNITED STATES OF AMERICA

Mediation is effectively a technique or group of techniques which have been imported from the North Americas. The USA, having a severe problem with litigation, had a need to develop less expensive methods of resolving disputes generally.

The techniques developed in the USA have been imported into the English jurisdiction and it has begun to benefit from them. However, the extent of its use has not reached the same level.

The USA lead the world in developing mediation

It can be said with considerable certainty that some of the techniques developed in the USA do not have the ability to be imported into the English system but, notwithstanding this, most of the techniques can be successfully transposed.

Mediation in the USA is a well accepted mode of resolving disputes and mediators are recognised as being crucial in most spheres where litigation exists.

The American States which have decided to provide support fully recognise the status and also provide a system of court registration of agreements obtained through mediation.

Arbitration is even more widely accepted and although it varies from State to State it has a level of acceptance which exceeds that in the United Kingdom.

There are a number of States which have specifically introduced legislation onto the statute book to provide the same type of support to mediation as the law previously gave to arbitration.

It is not until the courts in England apply penalties in costs to parties who do not take the process seriously that mediation will become as well accepted as it is in the USA.

In the USA there are three States which have very formalised use of ADR: California, Texas and New York. The need for ADR stems from the prolific use of litigation.

The field of employment law has also encouraged the inclusion of mediation and arbitration clauses. The courts maintain a supervisory role, as would be expected.

If an arbitration agreement is invoked, its award is enforceable through the courts. However, if the contract was signed 'under duress' it can be expected to be set aside.

One particular sphere in which lawyers have successfully set awards aside is in the health insurance field, where it was proved that the bargaining position of the parties was not equal and that the ability to avoid signing the agreement in the first place was subject to unfair and unreasonable duress. An example is a seriously ill patient being admitted to a hospital, being asked to sign a contract for treatment incorporating a waiver to his right to commence litigation, and an obligation to use arbitral proceedings.

This power of the courts to set aside an award on grounds of the contract terms leading to the arbitration itself, is reflected in the Unfair Terms in Consumer Contracts Regulations 1994 in England, the terms of which have been incorporated in s 89 of the Arbitration Act 1996.

This having been said, the presumption is that an arbitral decision is binding on all the parties.

California is forefront in cases of medical negligence dealt with under the terms of arbitration agreements. Hand in hand with this is the use of mediation which means that most cases never actually reach an adjudication by an arbitrator even though the process is invoked and proceedings commenced.

Mediation is frequently incorporated as an adjunct to both arbitration and litigation. It is here that the differences between States become more pertinent. In those States where there is provision for registration of the mediated agreement with the court, the enforceability of the agreement is much stronger than in other States where the resulting contract provides the legal profession with fertile ground for increasing their remuneration.

The way in which mediation is used in the USA differs in a number of ways and shows the willingness of parties, if not the enthusiasm, not to become embroiled in prolonged contention.

A specific means of resolving major disputes by mediation

An example of a method of resolving disputes is shown in the following tribunal method. The method is appropriate to corporate disputes and relies upon the fact that in most organisations disputes are handled by upper-middle grade executives. These executives suffer from the fact that they are looking for promotion and, if a matter which they are charged with handling stagnates or alternatively 'goes seriously wrong', they have a vested interest in hiding their 'mistake'.

Once the dispute has reached this stage and positions are entrenched, mediation may be difficult to invoke, the parties being unwilling to give in.

The mediator thus invites a senior officer from each party's firm to attend a mediation at which the senior officers sit as a tribunal with the mediator chairing it. The executives who previously had the conduct of the case, act as advocates for their cause and address the tribunal as to the merits of their position.

Once this is done, the tribunal retires with the mediator. The senior persons should have a good knowledge of the issues and are senior enough to work a settlement aided by the mediator. Because the members of the tribunal are not 'watching over their shoulders' and are senior enough and knowledgeable enough to decide the matter, this method of resolving disputes has an even greater chance of resolving the matter than what might be termed 'ordinary methods of mediation'.

The insurers' influence

It is probably fair to say that the insurance companies have had more influence than any other group on the progress of alternative methods of resolving disputes.

Their influence is used because the cost of litigation has got out of hand in the States and it is the insurers who have to pay the bill. Ultimately this leads to an increase in insurance premiums.

SOUTH AFRICA

South Africa is, in terms of medical disputes and their resolution, a most interesting jurisdiction. The country is set to become very prominent in the field and thus its influence upon the future of dispute resolution procedures should not be underestimated.

Having a strong link to English common law and accepting some of the English judgments as precedent, it differs from the USA.

The current legislation covering arbitrations is the Arbitration Act 1965. The terms of the Act apply only to written agreements, and oral agreements remain enforceable under common law.

The current law is under review and there is a move to incorporate the UNCITRAL model law in the country's statute book.

There are several companies dedicated to the promotion of alternative means of resolving disputes, and there is a company which specialises in mediation, conciliation and arbitration of labour disputes. A similar company exists to resolve marine disputes.

The commercial world actively and widely uses arbitration as a means of resolving disputes.

The use of ADR in medical disputes, either personal injury or medical negligence, is not yet established, but there is no doubt with commercial progress such disputes will soon be considered for resolution outside the courts and the current legislative framework is already there for arbitrations. Mediation is already accepted and being practised which means that the jurisdiction is no novice to such methods, and there are many whose experience and sympathy for the techniques will allow them to flourish.

One organisation which is promoting alternative methods of resolving disputes in South Africa is the Alternative Dispute Resolution Association of South Africa. This organisation is predominant in providing ADR services within the country, mainly within the area of Johannesburg.

AUSTRALIA

Australia is a common law country in the mould of English common law, although it is not bound for the greater part by English legal precedents.

Australia, being a federation, has two main levels of law-making. The first is the Commonwealth of Australia which, like the National Government of the USA, controls and legislates matters which require the supra State control.

Arbitration is dealt with at State level and all the States have revised their Arbitration Laws since 1984. The legislation in all cases is termed 'Commercial Arbitration law'. It is of interest that, until the passage of this legislation, most arbitrations were in respect of building and construction disputes. This is beginning to change and federal courts legislation was passed permitting the court to refer disputes or parts of disputes to arbitration.

Australia has adopted the 1958 New York Convention which has grossly expedited the use of arbitration.

Whilst arbitration has become widely accepted, and mediation has been acknowledged, the use of both procedures is currently restricted predominantly to commercial matters, although some family mediation does take place. The use of arbitration in the sphere of medical disputes has not gained any significant level of acceptance.

In New South Wales, the government has taken a lead in promoting alternative methods of resolving disputes. ADR is now compulsory under a number of statutes as exemplified by the Farm Debt Mediation Act 1994, the Retail Leases Act 1994, the Family Law Act 1975 and the Courts Legislation (Mediation and Evaluation) Amendment Act 1994.

In May 1996, a federal government justice statement relating to family and community justice did much to advance the cause.

It is of note that the New South Wales Law Society, together with those of most of the other Australian States, have done much to enhance the use of alternative methods of resolving disputes.

The approach of the courts to mediation clauses in contracts is not yet certain. There is a tendency to support such clauses but there is also a tendency to view the process as being a voluntary one and thus not subject to an order of the court. The general tendency has, however, been to support such clauses as is demonstrated in *AWA Limited v George Richard Daniels t/a Deloitte and others* (1992) (Supreme Court of New South Wales) which decided that, in an effort for the court to control any abuse of process, the contractual provisions for conciliation should be complied with.

In *Hooper Baillie Associated Limited v Natcon Group Pty Limited & Anor* (1992), in the face of a clause in the parties' agreement to conciliate, it was decided that the arbitration would be stayed until conciliation proceedings were concluded.

In *Capolingua v Phylum Pty Limited* (1991), the Supreme Court found that where a party to a mediation adopted an obstructive attitude to narrowing the issues, and where it was shown that but for such conduct the issues would have been reduced, the courts may consider, when deciding issues of costs, the conduct of the parties in respect of the mediation.

The opinion presently prevailing is that such clauses should provide certainty if they are to be enforceable but that if that certainty is implied the clause will be upheld. Certainty relates to the ability to assign a sufficiently precise and clear meaning to the language used, allowing a court to identify the rights and obligations between the parties.

Sir Laurence Street, former New South Wales Chief Justice has, since retiring from the Bench, become very active as a commercial mediator. He says that he ascribes the acceptability of the process to a number of points, one of the most significant being that it provides the parties with certainty that they will not lose litigation. Parties are not in the position of winning a trial but losing a contract. His success is said to be in excess of 90%, which would be the norm for a competent mediator. He notes that most of his mediations last only a day and that his fee is commensurate with a senior Queen's Counsel.

There is a move afoot to ensure regulation of mediators since at present there is no such accreditation available.

The Victorian county court has taken the lead in setting up a scheme for the resolution of cases by mediation. The average dispute is now settled in under two months and at a cost of $3,000. The level of cases dealt with by the court is up to $100,000. Commenting on the success of the project, Judge Keon-Cohen is noted as having said that 'over 50% of cases desperate not to go to mediation settled under it'. He estimated that it cost six times as much to follow the traditional course of litigation as to settle through mediation.

It is, however, early in the genesis of the system and thus probably too early to make serious comment as to how it will proceed.

One major organisation involved in the advancement of ADR is the Australian Commercial Disputes Centre, which was founded in 1986. The organisation promotes all means of ADR including mediation, arbitration, expert determination and recommendation.

The organisation has compiled a number of clauses for use in contracts. It is not intended to reproduce these standard clauses in this book and the reader who is interested can seek details from the ACDC in Sydney.

Section 27 Commercial Arbitration Act 1984

27 – ... that the parties to an arbitration agreement may seek settlement of a dispute by mediation, conciliation or similar means, or may authorise an arbitrator or umpire to act as a mediator or conciliator or other non-arbitral intermediary. Further, if the mediation or conciliation fails to produce a settlement, no objection shall be taken to the conduct by the arbitrator of the subsequent arbitration on the grounds that the arbitrator had previously taken that action in relation to the dispute.

NEW ZEALAND

Arbitration has a long history of recognition in New Zealand; the first Act was published in 1908. This Act was later amended in 1938, and this law is the current law governing domestic arbitrations. International arbitrations are governed by the Arbitration Act 1983, in which the New York Convention was ratified.

Arbitration has been widely used in a variety of fields including governmental and major professional bodies' draft contracts, and the New Zealand Institute of Professional Engineers. Other spheres in which it has been used to great effect include valuation of property and partnership disputes.

The sphere of medical disputes has not been overtly using arbitration, and the current legislation covering medical negligence and no-fault systems for resolving the issues means that it is not likely to utilise arbitration until the present system changes radically. Mediation does not have a prominent place in the resolution of disputes either.

Since no records are kept of arbitrations undertaken, the compilation of figures and facts is somewhat inhibited.

SINGAPORE

Singapore is a major centre of commerce in the Far East and this is reflected by its adoption of laws to support the arbitral process. Its laws closely reflect the Arbitration Acts 1950–79.

It is recorded that very few arbitrations have taken place within the jurisdiction and this almost certainly reflects the true position. However, it should be borne in mind that by its very nature it is not possible to be sure of the number and outcome of disputes submitted to arbitration.

There is no immediately available information as to whether mediation is used within the country, but the suggestion is that it has yet to gain a foothold.

THE UNCITRAL ARBITRATION RULES

GENERAL ASSEMBLY RESOLUTION 31/98
UNCITRAL ARBITRATION RULES

RESOLUTION 31/98 ADOPTED BY THE GENERAL ASSEMBLY ON 15 DECEMBER 1976

31/98 – Arbitration Rules of the United Nations Commission on International Trade Law

The General Assembly:

Recognising the value of arbitration as a method of settling disputes arising in the context of international commercial relations;

Being convinced that the establishment of rules for *ad hoc* arbitration that are acceptable in countries with different legal, social and economic systems would significantly contribute to the development of harmonious international economic relations;

Bearing in mind that the Arbitration Rules of the United Nations Commission on International Trade Law have been prepared after extensive consultation with arbitral institutions and centres of international commercial arbitration;

Noting that the Arbitration Rules were adopted by the United Nations Commission on International Trade Law at its ninth session[1] after due deliberation;

1. Recommends the use of the Arbitration Rules of the United Nations Commission on International Trade Law in the settlement of disputes arising in the context of international commercial relations, particularly by reference to the Arbitration Rules in commercial contracts;

2. Requests the Secretary-General to arrange for the widest possible distribution of the Arbitration Rules.

---

1   Official Records of the General Assembly, Thirty-first Session, Supplement No 17 (A/31/17), chap V, sect C.

SECTION I – INTRODUCTORY RULES
Scope of application
Article 1

1. Where the parties to a contract have agreed in writing* that disputes in relation to that contract shall be referred to arbitration under the UNCITRAL Arbitration Rules, then such disputes shall be settled in accordance with these Rules subject to such modification as the parties may agree in writing.
2. These Rules shall govern the arbitration except that where any of these Rules is in conflict with a provision of the law applicable to the arbitration from which the parties cannot derogate, that provision shall prevail.

* MODEL ARBITRATION CLAUSE

Any dispute, controversy or claim arising out of or relating to this contract, or the breach, termination or invalidity thereof, shall be settled by arbitration in accordance with the UNCITRAL Arbitration Rules as at present in force.

Note – Parties may wish to consider adding:

(a) The appointing authority shall be ... (name of institution or person);
(b) The number of arbitrators shall be ... (one or three);
(c) The place of arbitration shall be ... (town or country);
(d) The language(s) to be used in the arbitral proceedings shall be ... .

Notice, calculation of periods of time
Article 2

1. For the purposes of these Rules, any notice, including a notification, communication or proposal, is deemed to have been received if it is physically delivered to the addressee or if it is delivered at his habitual residence, place of business or mailing address, or, if none of these can be found after making reasonable inquiry, then at the addressee's last known residence or place of business. Notice shall be deemed to have been received on the day it is so delivered.
2. For the purposes of calculating a period of time under these Rules, such period shall begin to run on the day following the day when a notice, notification, communication or proposal is received. If the last day of such period is an official holiday or a non-business day at the residence or place of business of the addressee, the period is extended until the first business day which follows. Official holidays or non-business days occurring during the running of the period of time are included in calculating the period.

Notice of arbitration

Article 3

1. The party initiating recourse to arbitration (hereinafter called the 'claimant') shall give to the other party (hereinafter called the 'respondent') a notice of arbitration.

2. Arbitral proceedings shall be deemed to commence on the date on which the notice of arbitration is received by the respondent.

3. The notice of arbitration shall include the following:

    (a) A demand that the dispute be referred to arbitration;
    (b) The names and addresses of the parties;
    (c) A reference to the arbitration clause or the separate arbitration agreement that is invoked;
    (d) A reference to the contract out of or in relation to which the dispute arises;
    (e) The general nature of the claim and an indication of the amount involved, if any;
    (f) The relief or remedy sought;
    (g) A proposal as to the number of arbitrators (ie one or three), if the parties have not previously agreed thereon.

4. The notice of arbitration may also include:

    (a) The proposals for the appointments of a sole arbitrator and an appointing authority referred to in Article 6, paragraph 1;
    (b) The notification of the appointment of an arbitrator referred to in Article 7;
    (c) The statement of claim referred to in Article 18.

Representation and assistance

Article 4

The parties may be represented or assisted by persons of their choice. The names and addresses of such persons must be communicated in writing to the other party; such communication must specify whether the appointment is being made for purposes of representation or assistance.

SECTION II – COMPOSITION OF THE ARBITRAL TRIBUNAL

Number of arbitrators

Article 5

If the parties have not previously agreed on the number of arbitrators (ie one or three), and if within 15 days after the receipt by the respondent of the notice of arbitration the parties have not agreed that there shall be only one arbitrator, three arbitrators shall be appointed.

Appointment of arbitrators (Articles 6–8)

Article 6

1. If a sole arbitrator is to be appointed, either party may propose to the other:
   (a) The names of one or more persons, one of whom would serve as the sole arbitrator; and
   (b) If no appointing authority has been agreed upon by the parties, the name or names of one or more institutions or persons, one of whom would serve as appointing authority.

2. If within 30 days after receipt by a party of a proposal made in accordance with paragraph 1 the parties have not reached agreement on the choice of a sole arbitrator, the sole arbitrator shall be appointed by the appointing authority agreed upon by the parties. If no appointing authority has been agreed upon by the parties, or if the appointing authority agreed upon refuses to act or fails to appoint the arbitrator within 60 days of the receipt of a party's request therefore, either party may request the Secretary-General of the Permanent Court of Arbitration at The Hague to designate an appointing authority.

3. The appointing authority shall, at the request of one of the parties, appoint the sole arbitrator as promptly as possible. In making the appointment the appointing authority shall use the following list procedure, unless both parties agree that the list procedure should not be used or unless the appointing authority determines in its discretion that the use of the list procedure is not appropriate for the case:
   (a) At the request of one of the parties the appointing authority shall communicate to both parties an identical list containing at least three names;
   (b) Within 15 days after the receipt of his list, each party may return the list to the appointing authority after having deleted the name or names to which he objects and numbered the remaining names on the list in the order of his preference;
   (c) After the expiration of the above period of time the appointing authority shall appoint the sole arbitrator from among the names

approved on the lists returned to it and in accordance with the order of preference indicated by the parties;

(d) If for any reason the appointment cannot be made according to this procedure, the appointing authority may exercise its discretion in appointing the sole arbitrator.

4.   In making the appointment, the appointing authority shall have regard to such considerations as are likely to secure the appointment of an independent and impartial arbitrator and shall take into account as well the advisability of appointing an arbitrator of a nationality other than the nationalities of the parties.

Article 7

1.   If three arbitrators are to be appointed, each party shall appoint one arbitrator. The two arbitrators thus appointed shall choose the third arbitrator who will act as the presiding arbitrator of the tribunal.

2.   If within 30 days after the receipt of a party's notification of the appointment of an arbitrator the other party has not notified the first party of the arbitrator he has appointed:

(a) The first party may request the appointing authority previously designated by the parties to appoint the second arbitrator; or

(b) If no such authority has been previously designated by the parties, or if the appointing authority previously designated refuses to act or fails to appoint the arbitrator within 30 days after receipt of a party's request therefore, the first party may request the Secretary-General of the Permanent Court of Arbitration at The Hague to designate the appointing authority. The first party may then request the appointing authority so designated to appoint the second arbitrator. In either case, the appointing authority may exercise its discretion in appointing the arbitrator.

3.   If within 30 days after the appointment of the second arbitrator, the two arbitrators have not agreed on the choice of the presiding arbitrator, the presiding arbitrator shall be appointed by an appointing authority in the same way as a sole arbitrator would be appointed under Article 6.

Article 8

1.   When an appointing authority is requested to appoint an arbitrator pursuant to Article 6 or 7, the party which makes the request shall send to the appointing authority a copy of the notice of arbitration, a copy of the contract out of or in relation to which the dispute has arisen and a copy of the arbitration agreement if it is not contained in the contract. The appointing authority may require from either party such information as it deems necessary to fulfil its function.

2. Where the names of one or more persons are proposed for appointment as arbitrators, their full names, addresses and nationalities shall be indicated, together with a description of their qualifications.

Challenge of arbitrators (Articles 9–12)

Article 9

A prospective arbitrator shall disclose to those who approach him in connection with his possible appointment, any circumstances likely to give rise to justifiable doubts as to his impartiality or independence. An arbitrator, once appointed or chosen, shall disclose such circumstances to the parties unless they have already been informed by him of these circumstances.

Article 10

1. Any arbitrator may be challenged if circumstances exist that give rise to justifiable doubts as to the arbitrator's impartiality or independence.
2. A party may challenge the arbitrator appointed by him only for reasons of which he becomes aware after the appointment has been made.

Article 11

1. A party who intends to challenge an arbitrator shall send notice of his challenge within 15 days after the appointment of the challenged arbitrator has been notified to the challenging party or within 15 days after the circumstances mentioned in Articles 9 and 10 became known to that party.
2. The challenge shall be notified to the other party, to the arbitrator who is challenged and to the other members of the arbitral tribunal. The notification shall be in writing and shall state the reasons for the challenge.
3. When an arbitrator has been challenged by one party, the other party may agree to the challenge. The arbitrator may also, after the challenge, withdraw from his office. In neither case does this imply acceptance of the validity of the grounds for the challenge. In both cases the procedure provided in Article 6 or 7 shall be used in full for the appointment of the substitute arbitrator, even if during the process of appointing the challenged arbitrator a party had failed to exercise his right to appoint or to participate in the appointment.

Article 12

1. If the other party does not agree to the challenge and the challenged arbitrator does not withdraw, the decision on the challenge will be made:

   (a) When the initial appointment was made by an appointing authority, by that authority;

   (b) When the initial appointment was not made by an appointing authority, but an appointing authority has been previously designated, by that authority;

   (c) In all other cases, by the appointing authority to be designated in accordance with the procedure for designating an appointing authority as provided for in Article 6.

2. If the appointing authority sustains the challenge, a substitute arbitrator shall be appointed or chosen pursuant to the procedure applicable to the appointment or choice of an arbitrator as provided in Articles 6–9 except that, when this procedure would call for the designation of an appointing authority, the appointment of the arbitrator shall be made by the appointing authority which decided on the challenge.

Replacement of an arbitrator

Article 13

1. In the event of the death or resignation of an arbitrator during the course of the arbitral proceedings, a substitute arbitrator shall be appointed or chosen pursuant to the procedure provided for in Articles 6–9 that was applicable to the appointment or choice of the arbitrator being replaced.

2. In the event that an arbitrator fails to act or in the event of the *de jure* or *de facto* impossibility of his performing his functions, the procedure in respect of the challenge and replacement of an arbitrator as provided in the preceding Articles shall apply.

Repetition of hearings in the event of the replacement of an arbitrator

Article 14

If under Articles 11–13 the sole or presiding arbitrator is replaced, any hearings held previously shall be repeated; if any other arbitrator is replaced, such prior hearings may be repeated at the discretion of the arbitral tribunal.

SECTION III – ARBITRAL PROCEEDINGS

General provisions

Article 15

1. Subject to these Rules, the arbitral tribunal may conduct the arbitration in such manner as it considers appropriate, provided that the parties are

treated with equality and that at any stage of the proceedings each party is given a full opportunity of presenting his case.

2. If either party so requests at any stage of the proceedings, the arbitral tribunal shall hold hearings for the presentation of evidence by witnesses, including expert witnesses, or for oral argument. In the absence of such a request, the arbitral tribunal shall decide whether to hold such hearings or whether the proceedings shall be conducted on the basis of documents and other materials.

3. All documents or information supplied to the arbitral tribunal by one party shall at the same time be communicated by that party to the other party.

Place of arbitration

Article 16

1. Unless the parties have agreed upon the place where the arbitration is to be held, such place shall be determined by the arbitral tribunal, having regard to the circumstances of the arbitration.

2. The arbitral tribunal may determine the locale of the arbitration within the country agreed upon by the parties. It may hear witnesses and hold meetings for consultation among its members at any place it deems appropriate, having regard to the circumstances of the arbitration.

3. The arbitral tribunal may meet at any place it deems appropriate for the inspection of goods, other property or documents. The parties shall be given sufficient notice to enable them to be present at such inspection.

4. The award shall be made at the place of arbitration.

Language

Article 17

1. Subject to an agreement by the parties, the arbitral tribunal shall, promptly after its appointment, determine the language or languages to be used in the proceedings. This determination shall apply to the statement of claim, the statement of defence, and any further written statements and, if oral hearings take place, to the language or languages to be used in such hearings.

2. The arbitral tribunal may order that any documents annexed to the statement of claim or statement of defence, and any supplementary documents or exhibits submitted in the course of the proceedings, delivered in their original language, shall be accompanied by a translation into the language or languages agreed upon by the parties or determined by the arbitral tribunal.

Statement of claim

Article 18

1. Unless the statement of claim was contained in the notice of arbitration, within a period of time to be determined by the arbitral tribunal, the claimant shall communicate his statement of claim in writing to the respondent and to each of the arbitrators. A copy of the contract, and of the arbitration agreement, if not contained in the contract, shall be annexed thereto.

2. The statement of claim shall include the following particulars:

   (a) The names and addresses of the parties;

   (b) A statement of the facts supporting the claim;

   (c) The points at issue;

   (d) The relief or remedy sought.

   The claimant may annex to his statement of claim all documents he deems relevant or may add a reference to the documents or other evidence he will submit.

Statement of defence

Article 19

1. Within a period of time to be determined by the arbitral tribunal, the respondent shall communicate his statement of defence in writing to the claimant and to each of the arbitrators.

2. The statement of defence shall reply to the particulars (b), (c) and (d) of the statement of claim (Article 18, paragraph 2). The respondent may annex to his statement the documents on which he relies for his defence or may add a reference to the documents or other evidence he will submit.

3. In his statement of defence or at a later stage in the arbitral proceedings, if the arbitral tribunal decides that the delay was justified under the circumstances, the respondent may make a counterclaim arising out of the same contract or rely on a claim arising out of the same contract for the purpose of a setoff.

4. The provisions of Article 18, paragraph 2, shall apply to a counterclaim and a claim relied on for the purpose of a setoff.

Amendments to the claim or defence

Article 20

During the course of the arbitral proceedings either party may amend or supplement his claim or defence unless the arbitral tribunal considers it inappropriate to allow such amendment having regard to the delay in making it or prejudice to the other party or any other circumstances. However, a claim may not be amended in such a manner that the amended claim falls outside the scope of the arbitration clause or separate arbitration agreement.

Pleas as to the jurisdiction of the arbitral tribunal
Article 21

1. The arbitral tribunal shall have the power to rule on objections that it has no jurisdiction, including any objections with respect to the existence or validity of the arbitration clause or of the separate arbitration agreement.
2. The arbitral tribunal shall have the power to determine the existence or the validity of the contract of which an arbitration clause forms a part. For the purposes of Article 21, an arbitration clause which forms part of a contract and which provides for arbitration under these Rules shall be treated as an agreement independent of the other terms of the contract. A decision by the arbitral tribunal that the contract is null and void shall not entail *ipso jure* the invalidity of the arbitration clause.
3. A plea that the arbitral tribunal does not have jurisdiction shall be raised not later than in the statement of defence or, with respect to a counterclaim, in the reply to the counterclaim.
4. In general, the arbitral tribunal should rule on a plea concerning its jurisdiction as a preliminary question. However, the arbitral tribunal may proceed with the arbitration and rule on such a plea in their final award.

Further written statements
Article 22

The arbitral tribunal shall decide which further written statements, in addition to the statement of claim and the statement of defence, shall be required from the parties or may be presented by them and shall fix the periods of time for communicating such statements.

Periods of time
Article 23

The periods of time fixed by the arbitral tribunal for the communication of written statements (including the statement of claim and statement of defence) should not exceed 45 days. However, the arbitral tribunal may extend the time limits if it concludes that an extension is justified.

Evidence and hearings (Articles 24–25)
Article 24

1. Each party shall have the burden of proving the facts relied on to support his claim or defence.

2. The arbitral tribunal may, if it considers it appropriate, require a party to deliver to the tribunal and to the other party, within such a period of time as the arbitral tribunal shall decide, a summary of the documents and other evidence which that party intends to present in support of the facts in issue set out in his statement of claim or statement of defence.

3. At any time during the arbitral proceedings the arbitral tribunal may require the parties to produce documents, exhibits or other evidence within such a period of time as the tribunal shall determine.

Article 25

1. In the event of an oral hearing, the arbitral tribunal shall give the parties adequate advance notice of the date, time and place thereof.

2. If witnesses are to be heard, at least 15 days before the hearing each party shall communicate to the arbitral tribunal and to the other party, the names and addresses of the witnesses he intends to present, the subject upon and the languages in which such witnesses will give their testimony.

3. The arbitral tribunal shall make arrangements for the translation of oral statements made at a hearing and for a record of the hearing if either is deemed necessary by the tribunal under the circumstances of the case, or if the parties have agreed thereto and have communicated such agreement to the tribunal at least 15 days before the hearing.

4. Hearings shall be held in camera unless the parties agree otherwise. The arbitral tribunal may require the retirement of any witness or witnesses during the testimony of other witnesses. The arbitral tribunal is free to determine the manner in which witnesses are examined.

5. Evidence of witnesses may also be presented in the form of written statements signed by them.

6. The arbitral tribunal shall determine the admissibility, relevance, materiality and weight of the evidence offered.

Interim measures of protection

Article 26

1. At the request of either party, the arbitral tribunal may take any interim measures it deems necessary in respect of the subject-matter of the dispute, including measures for the conservation of the goods forming the subject-matter in dispute, such as ordering their deposit with a third person or the sale of perishable goods.

2. Such interim measures may be established in the form of an interim award. The arbitral tribunal shall be entitled to require security for the costs of such measures.

3. A request for interim measures addressed by any party to a judicial authority shall not be deemed incompatible with the agreement to arbitrate, or as a waiver of that agreement.

Experts

Article 27

1. The arbitral tribunal may appoint one or more experts to report to it, in writing, on specific issues to be determined by the tribunal. A copy of the experts terms of reference, established by the arbitral tribunal, shall be communicated to the parties.

2. The parties shall give the expert any relevant information or produce for his inspection any relevant documents or goods that he may require of them. Any dispute between a party and such expert as to the relevance of the required information or production shall be referred to the arbitral tribunal for decision.

3. Upon receipt of the expert's report, the arbitral tribunal shall communicate a copy of the report to the parties who shall be given the opportunity to express, in writing, their opinion on the report. A party shall be entitled to examine any document on which the expert has relied in his report.

4. At the request of either party the expert, after delivery of the report, may be heard at a hearing where the parties shall have the opportunity to be present and to interrogate the expert. At this hearing either party may present expert witnesses in order to testify on the points at issue. The provisions of Article 25 shall be applicable to such proceedings.

Default

Article 28

1. If, within the period of time fixed by the arbitral tribunal, the claimant has failed to communicate his claim without showing sufficient cause for such failure, the arbitral tribunal shall issue an order for the termination of the arbitral proceedings. If, within the period of time fixed by the arbitral tribunal, the respondent has failed to communicate his statement of defence without showing sufficient cause for such failure, the arbitral tribunal shall order that the proceedings continue.

2. If one of the parties, duly notified under these Rules, fails to appear at a hearing, without showing sufficient cause for such failure, the arbitral tribunal may proceed with the arbitration.

3. If one of the parties, duly invited to produce documentary evidence, fails to do so within the established period of time, without showing sufficient cause for such failure, the arbitral tribunal may make the award on the evidence before it.

Closure of hearings

Article 29

1. The arbitral tribunal may inquire of the parties if they have any further proof to offer or witnesses to be heard or submissions to make and, if there are none, it may declare the hearings closed.

2. The arbitral tribunal may, if it considers it necessary owing to exceptional circumstances, decide, on its own motion or upon application of a party, to reopen the hearings at any time before the award is made.

Waiver of rules

Article 30

A party who knows that any provision of, or requirement under, these Rules has not been complied with and yet proceeds with the arbitration without promptly stating his objection to such non-compliance, shall be deemed to have waived his right to object.

SECTION IV – THE AWARD

Decisions

Article 31

1. When there are three arbitrators, any award or other decision of the arbitral tribunal shall be made by a majority of the arbitrators.

2. In the case of questions of procedure, when there is no majority or when the arbitral tribunal so authorises, the presiding arbitrator may decide on his own, subject to revision, if any, by the arbitral tribunal.

Form and effect of the award

Article 32

1. In addition to making a final award, the arbitral tribunal shall be entitled to make interim, interlocutory, or partial awards.

2. The award shall be made in writing and shall be final and binding on the parties. The parties undertake to carry out the award without delay.

3. The arbitral tribunal shall state the reasons upon which the award is based, unless the parties have agreed that no reasons are to be given.

4. An award shall be signed by the arbitrators and it shall contain the date on which and the place where the award was made. Where there are three arbitrators and one of them fails to sign, the award shall state the reason for the absence of the signature.

5. The award may be made public only with the consent of both parties.

6. Copies of the award signed by the arbitrators shall be communicated to the parties by the arbitral tribunal.

7. If the arbitration law of the country where the award is made requires that the award be filed or registered by the arbitral tribunal, the tribunal shall comply with this requirement within the period of time required by law.

Applicable law, *amiable compositeur*

Article 33

1. The arbitral tribunal shall apply the law designated by the parties as applicable to the substance of the dispute. Failing such designation by the parties, the arbitral tribunal shall apply the law determined by the conflict of laws rules which it considers applicable.

2. The arbitral tribunal shall decide as *amiable compositeur* or *ex aequo et bono* only if the parties have expressly authorised the arbitral tribunal to do so and if the law applicable to the arbitral procedure permits such arbitration.

3. In all cases, the arbitral tribunal shall decide in accordance with the terms of the contract and shall take into account the usages of the trade applicable to the transaction.

Settlement or other grounds for termination

Article 34

1. If, before the award is made, the parties agree on a settlement of the dispute, the arbitral tribunal shall either issue an order for the termination of the arbitral proceedings or, if requested by both parties and accepted by the tribunal, record the settlement in the form of an arbitral award on agreed terms. The arbitral tribunal is not obliged to give reasons for such an award.

2. If, before the award is made, the continuation of the arbitral proceedings becomes unnecessary or impossible for any reason not mentioned in paragraph 1, the arbitral tribunal shall inform the parties of its intention to issue an order for the termination of the proceedings. The arbitral tribunal shall have the power to issue such an order unless a party raises justifiable grounds for objection.

3. Copies of the order for termination of the arbitral proceedings or of the arbitral award on agreed terms, signed by the arbitrators, shall be communicated by the arbitral tribunal to the parties. Where an arbitral award on agreed terms is made, the provisions of Article 32, paragraphs 2 and 4–7, shall apply.

Interpretation of the award

Article 35

1. Within 30 days after the receipt of the award, either party, with notice to the other party, may request that the arbitral tribunal give an interpretation of the award.

2. The interpretation shall be given in writing within 45 days after the receipt of the request. The interpretation shall form part of the award and the provisions of Article 32, paragraphs 2–7, shall apply.

Correction of the award

Article 36

1. Within 30 days after the receipt of the award, either party, with notice to the other party, may request the arbitral tribunal to correct in the award any errors in computation, any clerical or typographical errors, or any errors of similar nature. The arbitral tribunal may within 30 days after the communication of the award make such corrections on its own initiative.

2. Such corrections shall be in writing, and the provisions of Article 32, paragraphs 2–7, shall apply.

Additional award

Article 37

1. Within 30 days after the receipt of the award, either party, with notice to the other party, may request the arbitral tribunal to make an additional award as to claims presented in the arbitral proceedings but omitted from the award.

2. If the arbitral tribunal considers the request for an additional award to be justified and considers that the omission can be rectified without any further hearings or evidence, it shall complete its award within 60 days after the receipt of the request.

3. When an additional award is made, the provisions of Article 32, paragraphs 2–7, shall apply.

Costs (Articles 38–40)

Article 38

The arbitral tribunal shall fix the costs of arbitration in its award. The term 'costs' includes only:

(a) The fees of the arbitral tribunal to be stated separately as to each arbitrator and to be fixed by the tribunal itself in accordance with Article 39;

(b) The travel and other expenses incurred by the arbitrators;

(c) The costs of expert advice and of other assistance required by the arbitral tribunal;

(d) The travel and other expenses of witnesses to the extent such expenses are approved by the arbitral tribunal;

(e) The costs for legal representation and assistance of the successful party if such costs were claimed during the arbitral proceedings, and only to the extent that the arbitral tribunal determines that the amount of such costs is reasonable;

(f) Any fees and expenses of the appointing authority as well as the expenses of the Secretary-General of the Permanent Court of Arbitration at The Hague.

Article 39

1. The fees of the arbitral tribunal shall be reasonable in amount, taking into account the amount in dispute, the complexity of the subject-matter, the time spent by the arbitrators and any other relevant circumstances of the case.

2. If an appointing authority has been agreed upon by the parties or designated by the Secretary-General of the Permanent Court of Arbitration at The Hague, and if that authority has issued a schedule of fees for arbitrators in international cases which it administers, the arbitral tribunal in fixing its fees shall take that schedule of fees into account to the extent that it considers appropriate in the circumstances of the case.

3. If such appointing authority has not issued a schedule of fees for arbitrators in international cases, any party may at any time request the appointing authority to furnish a statement setting forth the basis for establishing fees which is customarily followed in international cases in which the authority appoints arbitrators. If the appointing authority consents to provide such a statement, the arbitral tribunal in fixing its fees shall take such information into account to the extent that it considers appropriate in the circumstances of the case.

4. In cases referred to in paragraphs 2 and 3, when a party so requests and the appointing authority consents to perform the function, the arbitral tribunal shall fix its fees only after consultation with the appointing authority which may make any comment it deems appropriate to the arbitral tribunal concerning the fees.

Article 40

1. Except as provided in paragraph 2, the costs of arbitration shall in principle be borne by the unsuccessful party. However, the arbitral tribunal may apportion each of such costs between the parties if it

determines that apportionment is reasonable, taking into account the circumstances of the case.

2. With respect to the costs of legal representation and assistance referred to in Article 38, paragraph (e), the arbitral tribunal, taking into account the circumstances of the case, shall be free to determine which party shall bear such costs or may apportion such costs between the parties if it determines that apportionment is reasonable.

3. When the arbitral tribunal issues an order for the termination of the arbitral proceedings or makes an award on agreed terms, it shall fix the costs of arbitration referred to in Article 38 and Article 39, paragraph 1, in the text of that order or award.

4. No additional fees may be charged by an arbitral tribunal for interpretation or correction or completion of its award under Articles 35–37.

Deposit of costs

Article 41

1. The arbitral tribunal, on its establishment, may request each party to deposit an equal amount as an advance for the costs referred to in Article 38, paragraphs (a), (b) and (c).

2. During the course of the arbitral proceedings, the arbitral tribunal may request supplementary deposits from the parties.

3. If an appointing authority has been agreed upon by the parties or designated by the Secretary-General of the Permanent Court of Arbitration at The Hague, and when a party so requests and the appointing authority consents to perform the function, the arbitral tribunal shall fix the amounts of any deposits or supplementary deposits only after consultation with the appointing authority which may make any comments to the arbitral tribunal which it deems appropriate concerning the amount of such deposits and supplementary deposits.

4. If the required deposits are not paid in full within 30 days after the receipt of the request, the arbitral tribunal shall so inform the parties in order that one or another of them may make the required payment. If such payment is not made, the arbitral tribunal may order the suspension or termination of the arbitral proceedings.

5. After the award has been made, the arbitral tribunal shall render an accounting to the parties of the deposits received and return any unexpended balance to the parties.

THE UNCITRAL MODEL LAW

UNCITRAL MODEL LAW ON

INTERNATIONAL COMMERCIAL ARBITRATION

UNITED NATIONS

1994

CONTENTS

EXPLANATORY NOTE BY THE UNCITRAL SECRETARIAT
ON THE MODEL LAW ON INTERNATIONAL COMMERCIAL
ARBITRATION

A   Background to the Model Law
   1   Inadequacy of domestic laws
   2   Disparity between national laws

B   Salient features of the Model Law
   1   Special procedural regime for international commercial arbitration
   2   Arbitration agreement
   3   Composition of arbitral tribunal
   4   Jurisdiction of arbitral tribunal
   5   Conduct of arbitral proceedings
   6   Making of award and termination of proceedings
   7   Recourse against award
   8   Recognition and enforcement of awards

UNCITRAL MODEL LAW ON INTERNATIONAL COMMERCIAL ARBITRATION

(United Nations document A/40/17, Annex I)

(As adopted by the United Nations Commission on International Trade Law on 21 June 1985)

CHAPTER I – GENERAL PROVISIONS

Scope of application*

Article 1

(1) This Law applies to international commercial** arbitration, subject to any agreement in force between this State and any other State or States.

(2) The provisions of this Law, except Articles 8, 9, 35 and 36, apply only if the place of arbitration is in the territory of this State.

(3) An arbitration is international if:

    (a) the parties to an arbitration agreement have, at the time of the conclusion of that agreement, their places of business in different States; or

    (b) one of the following places is situated outside the State in which the parties have their places of business:

        (i) the place of arbitration if determined in, or pursuant to, the arbitration agreement;

        (ii) any place where a substantial part of the obligations of the commercial relationship is to be performed or the place with which the subject-matter of the dispute is most closely connected; or

    (c) the parties have expressly agreed that the subject-matter of the arbitration agreement relates to more than one country.

(4) For the purposes of paragraph (3) of this Article:

    (a) if a party has more than one place of business, the place of business is that which has the closest relationship to the arbitration agreement;

    (b) if a party does not have a place of business, reference is to be made to his habitual residence.

---

*   Article headings are for reference purposes only and are not to be used for purposes of interpretation.

**   The term 'commercial' should be given a wide interpretation so as to cover matters arising from all relationships of a commercial nature, whether contractual or not. Relationships of a commercial nature include, but are not limited to, the following transactions: any trade transaction for the supply or exchange of goods or services; distribution agreement; commercial representation or agency; factoring; leasing; construction of works; consulting; engineering; licensing; investment; financing; banking; insurance; exploitation agreement or concession; joint venture and other forms of industrial or business cooperation; carriage of goods or passengers by air, sea, rail or road.

(5) This Law shall not affect any other law of this State by virtue of which certain disputes may not be submitted to arbitration or may be submitted to arbitration only according to provisions other than those of this Law.

Definitions and rules of interpretation
Article 2

For the purposes of this Law:

(a) 'arbitration' means any arbitration whether or not administered by a permanent arbitral institution;

(b) 'arbitral tribunal' means a sole arbitrator or a panel of arbitrators;

(c) 'court' means a body or organ of the judicial system of a State;

(d) where a provision of this Law, except Article 28, leaves the parties free to determine a certain issue, such freedom includes the right of the parties to authorise a third party, including an institution, to make that determination;

(e) where a provision of this Law refers to the fact that the parties have agreed or that they may agree or in any other way refers to an agreement of the parties, such agreement includes any arbitration rules referred to in that agreement;

(f) where a provision of this Law, other than in Articles 25(a) and 32(2)(a), refers to a claim, it also applies to a counterclaim, and where it refers to a defence, it also applies to a defence to such counterclaim.

Receipt of written communications
Article 3

(1) Unless otherwise agreed by the parties:

(a) any written communication is deemed to have been received if it is delivered to the addressee personally or if it is delivered at his place of business, habitual residence or mailing address; if none of these can be found after making a reasonable inquiry, a written communication is deemed to have been received if it is sent to the addressee's last known place of business, habitual residence or mailing address by registered letter or any other means which provides a record of the attempt to deliver it;

(b) the communication is deemed to have been received on the day it is so delivered.

(2) The provisions of this Article do not apply to communications in court proceedings.

Waiver of right to object

Article 4

A party who knows that any provision of this Law from which the parties may derogate or any requirement under the arbitration agreement has not been complied with and yet proceeds with the arbitration without stating his objection to such non-compliance without undue delay or, if a time limit is provided therefore, within such period of time, shall be deemed to have waived his right to object.

Extent of court intervention

Article 5

In matters governed by this Law, no court shall intervene except where so provided in this Law.

Court or other authority for certain functions of arbitration assistance and supervision

Article 6

The functions referred to in Articles 11(3), 11(4), 13(3), 14, 16(3) and 34(2) shall be performed by ... [Each State enacting this Model Law specifies the court, courts or, where referred to therein, other authority competent to perform these functions.]

CHAPTER II – ARBITRATION AGREEMENT

Definition and form of arbitration agreement

Article 7

(1) 'Arbitration agreement' is an agreement by the parties to submit to arbitration all or certain disputes which have arisen or which may arise between them in respect of a defined legal relationship, whether contractual or not. An arbitration agreement may be in the form of an arbitration clause in a contract or in the form of a separate agreement.

(2) The arbitration agreement shall be in writing. An agreement is in writing if it is contained in a document signed by the parties or in an exchange of letters, telex, telegrams or other means of telecommunication which provide a record of the agreement, or in an exchange of statements of claim and defence in which the existence of an agreement is alleged by one party and not denied by another. The reference in a contract to a document containing an arbitration clause constitutes an arbitration agreement provided that the contract is in writing and the reference is such as to make that clause part of the contract.

Arbitration agreement and substantive claim before court

Article 8

(1) A court before which an action is brought in a matter which is the subject of an arbitration agreement shall, if a party so requests, not later than when submitting his first statement on the substance of the dispute, refer the parties to arbitration unless it finds that the agreement is null and void, inoperative or incapable of being performed.

(2) Where an action referred to in paragraph (1) of this Article has been brought, arbitral proceedings may nevertheless be commenced or continued, and an award may be made, while the issue is pending before the court.

Arbitration agreement and interim measures by court

Article 9

It is not incompatible with an arbitration agreement for a party to request, before or during arbitral proceedings, from a court an interim measure of protection and for a court to grant such measure.

CHAPTER III – COMPOSITION OF ARBITRAL TRIBUNAL

Number of arbitrators

Article 10

(1) The parties are free to determine the number of arbitrators.

(2) Failing such determination, the number of arbitrators shall be three.

Appointment of arbitrators

Article 11

(1) No person shall be precluded by reason of his nationality from acting as an arbitrator, unless otherwise agreed by the parties.

(2) The parties are free to agree on a procedure of appointing the arbitrator or arbitrators, subject to the provisions of paragraphs (4) and (5) of this Article.

(3) Failing such agreement:

  (a) in an arbitration with three arbitrators, each party shall appoint one arbitrator, and the two arbitrators thus appointed shall appoint the third arbitrator; if a party fails to appoint the arbitrator within 30 days of receipt of a request to do so from the other party, or if the two arbitrators fail to agree on the third arbitrator within 30 days of their appointment, the appointment shall be made, upon request of a party, by the court or other authority specified in Article 6;

(b) in an arbitration with a sole arbitrator, if the parties are unable to agree on the arbitrator, he shall be appointed, upon request of a party, by the court or other authority specified in Article 6.

(4) Where, under an appointment procedure agreed upon by the parties:

(a) a party fails to act as required under such procedure; or

(b) the parties, or two arbitrators, are unable to reach an agreement expected of them under such procedure; or

(c) a third party, including an institution, fails to perform any function entrusted to it under such procedure,

any party may request the court or other authority specified in Article 6 to take the necessary measure, unless the agreement on the appointment procedure provides other means for securing the appointment.

(5) A decision on a matter entrusted by paragraph (3) or (4) of this Article to the court or other authority specified in Article 6 shall be subject to no appeal. The court or other authority, in appointing an arbitrator, shall have due regard to any qualifications required of the arbitrator by the agreement of the parties and to such considerations as are likely to secure the appointment of an independent and impartial arbitrator and, in the case of a sole or third arbitrator, shall take into account as well the advisability of appointing an arbitrator of a nationality other than those of the parties.

Grounds for challenge

Article 12

(1) When a person is approached in connection with his possible appointment as an arbitrator, he shall disclose any circumstances likely to give rise to justifiable doubts as to his impartiality or independence. An arbitrator, from the time of his appointment and throughout the arbitral proceedings, shall without delay disclose any such circumstances to the parties unless they have already been informed of them by him.

(2) An arbitrator may be challenged only if circumstances exist that give rise to justifiable doubts as to his impartiality or independence, or if he does not possess qualifications agreed to by the parties. A party may challenge an arbitrator appointed by him, or in whose appointment he has participated, only for reasons of which he becomes aware after the appointment has been made.

Challenge procedure

Article 13

(1) The parties are free to agree on a procedure for challenging an arbitrator, subject to the provisions of paragraph (3) of this Article.

(2) Failing such agreement, a party who intends to challenge an arbitrator shall, within 15 days after becoming aware of the constitution of the arbitral tribunal or after becoming aware of any circumstance referred to in Article 12(2), send a written statement of the reasons for the challenge to the arbitral tribunal. Unless the challenged arbitrator withdraws from his office or the other party agrees to the challenge, the arbitral tribunal shall decide on the challenge.

(3) If a challenge under any procedure agreed upon by the parties or under the procedure of paragraph (2) of this Article is not successful, the challenging party may request, within 30 days after having received notice of the decision rejecting the challenge, the court or other authority specified in Article 6 to decide on the challenge, which decision shall be subject to no appeal; while such a request is pending, the arbitral tribunal, including the challenged arbitrator, may continue the arbitral proceedings and make an award.

Failure or impossibility to act
Article 14

(1) If an arbitrator becomes *de jure* or *de facto* unable to perform his functions or for other reasons fails to act without undue delay, his mandate terminates if he withdraws from his office or if the parties agree on the termination. Otherwise, if a controversy remains concerning any of these grounds, any party may request the court or other authority specified in Article 6 to decide on the termination of the mandate, which decision shall be subject to no appeal.

(2) If, under this Article or Article 13(2), an arbitrator withdraws from his office or a party agrees to the termination of the mandate of an arbitrator, this does not imply acceptance of the validity of any ground referred to in this Article or Article 12(2).

Appointment of substitute arbitrator
Article 15

Where the mandate of an arbitrator terminates under Article 13 or 14 or because of his withdrawal from office for any other reason or because of the revocation of his mandate by agreement of the parties or in any other case of termination of his mandate, a substitute arbitrator shall be appointed according to the rules that were applicable to the appointment of the arbitrator being replaced.

CHAPTER IV – JURISDICTION OF ARBITRAL TRIBUNAL

Competence of arbitral tribunal to rule on its jurisdiction
Article 16

(1) The arbitral tribunal may rule on its own jurisdiction, including any objections with respect to the existence or validity of the arbitration agreement. For that purpose, an arbitration clause which forms part of a contract shall be treated as an agreement independent of the other terms of the contract. A decision by the arbitral tribunal that the contract is null and void shall not entail *ipso jure* the invalidity of the arbitration clause.

(2) A plea that the arbitral tribunal does not have jurisdiction shall be raised not later than the submission of the statement of defence. A party is not precluded from raising such a plea by the fact that he has appointed, or participated in the appointment of, an arbitrator. A plea that the arbitral tribunal is exceeding the scope of its authority shall be raised as soon as the matter alleged to be beyond the scope of its authority is raised during the arbitral proceedings. The arbitral tribunal may, in either case, admit a later plea if it considers the delay justified.

(3) The arbitral tribunal may rule on a plea referred to in paragraph (2) of this Article either as a preliminary question or in an award on the merits. If the arbitral tribunal rules as a preliminary question that it has jurisdiction, any party may request, within 30 days after having received notice of that ruling, the court specified in Article 6 to decide the matter, which decision shall be subject to no appeal; while such a request is pending, the arbitral tribunal may continue the arbitral proceedings and make an award.

Power of arbitral tribunal to order interim measures
Article 17

Unless otherwise agreed by the parties, the arbitral tribunal may, at the request of a party, order any party to take such interim measure of protection as the arbitral tribunal may consider necessary in respect of the subject-matter of the dispute. The arbitral tribunal may require any party to provide appropriate security in connection with such measure.

CHAPTER V – CONDUCT OF ARBITRAL PROCEEDINGS

Equal treatment of parties
Article 18

The parties shall be treated with equality and each party shall be given a full opportunity of presenting his case.

Determination of rules of procedure
Article 19

(1) Subject to the provisions of this Law, the parties are free to agree on the procedure to be followed by the arbitral tribunal in conducting the proceedings.

(2) Failing such agreement, the arbitral tribunal may, subject to the provisions of this Law, conduct the arbitration in such manner as it considers appropriate. The power conferred upon the arbitral tribunal includes the power to determine the admissibility, relevance, materiality and weight of any evidence.

Place of arbitration
Article 20

(1) The parties are free to agree on the place of arbitration. Failing such agreement, the place of arbitration shall be determined by the arbitral tribunal having regard to the circumstances of the case, including the convenience of the parties.

(2) Notwithstanding the provisions of paragraph (1) of this Article, the arbitral tribunal may, unless otherwise agreed by the parties, meet at any place it considers appropriate for consultation among its members, for hearing witnesses, experts or the parties, or for inspection of goods, other property or documents.

Commencement of arbitral proceedings
Article 21

Unless otherwise agreed by the parties, the arbitral proceedings in respect of a particular dispute commence on the date on which a request for that dispute to be referred to arbitration is received by the respondent.

Language
Article 22

(1) The parties are free to agree on the language or languages to be used in the arbitral proceedings. Failing such agreement, the arbitral tribunal shall determine the language or languages to be used in the proceedings. This agreement or determination, unless otherwise specified therein, shall apply to any written statement by a party, any hearing and any award, decision or other communication by the arbitral tribunal.

(2) The arbitral tribunal may order that any documentary evidence shall be accompanied by a translation into the language or languages agreed upon by the parties or determined by the arbitral tribunal.

Statements of claim and defence

Article 23

(1) Within the period of time agreed by the parties or determined by the arbitral tribunal, the claimant shall state the facts supporting his claim, the points at issue and the relief or remedy sought, and the respondent shall state his defence in respect of these particulars, unless the parties have otherwise agreed as to the required elements of such statements. The parties may submit with their statements all documents they consider to be relevant or may add a reference to the documents or other evidence they will submit.

(2) Unless otherwise agreed by the parties, either party may amend or supplement his claim or defence during the course of the arbitral proceedings, unless the arbitral tribunal considers it inappropriate to allow such amendment having regard to the delay in making it.

Hearings and written proceedings

Article 24

(1) Subject to any contrary agreement by the parties, the arbitral tribunal shall decide whether to hold oral hearings for the presentation of evidence or for oral argument, or whether the proceedings shall be conducted on the basis of documents and other materials. However, unless the parties have agreed that no hearings shall be held, the arbitral tribunal shall hold such hearings at an appropriate stage of the proceedings, if so requested by a party.

(2) The parties shall be given sufficient advance notice of any hearing and of any meeting of the arbitral tribunal for the purposes of inspection of goods, other property or documents.

(3) All statements, documents or other information supplied to the arbitral tribunal by one party shall be communicated to the other party. Also any expert report or evidentiary document on which the arbitral tribunal may rely in making its decision shall be communicated to the parties.

Default of a party

Article 25

Unless otherwise agreed by the parties, if, without showing sufficient cause:

(a) the claimant fails to communicate his statement of claim in accordance with Article 23(1), the arbitral tribunal shall terminate the proceedings;

(b) the respondent fails to communicate his statement of defence in accordance with Article 23(1), the arbitral tribunal shall continue the proceedings without treating such failure in itself as an admission of the claimant's allegations;

(c) any party fails to appear at a hearing or to produce documentary evidence, the arbitral tribunal may continue the proceedings and make the award on the evidence before it.

Expert appointed by arbitral tribunal
Article 26

(1) Unless otherwise agreed by the parties, the arbitral tribunal:

    (a) may appoint one or more experts to report to it on specific issues to be determined by the arbitral tribunal;

    (b) may require a party to give the expert any relevant information or to produce, or to provide access to, any relevant documents, goods or other property for his inspection.

(2) Unless otherwise agreed by the parties, if a party so requests or if the arbitral tribunal considers it necessary, the expert shall, after delivery of his written or oral report, participate in a hearing where the parties have the opportunity to put questions to him and to present expert witnesses in order to testify on the points at issue.

Court assistance in taking evidence
Article 27

The arbitral tribunal or a party with the approval of the arbitral tribunal may request from a competent court of this State assistance in taking evidence. The court may execute the request within its competence and according to its rules on taking evidence.

CHAPTER VI – MAKING OF AWARD AND TERMINATION OF PROCEEDINGS

Rules applicable to substance of dispute
Article 28

(1) The arbitral tribunal shall decide the dispute in accordance with such rules of law as are chosen by the parties as applicable to the substance of the dispute. Any designation of the law or legal system of a given State shall be construed, unless otherwise expressed, as directly referring to the substantive law of that State and not to its conflict of laws rules.

(2) Failing any designation by the parties, the arbitral tribunal shall apply the law determined by the conflict of laws rules which it considers applicable.

(3) The arbitral tribunal shall decide *ex aequo et bono* or as *amiable compositeur* only if the parties have expressly authorised it to do so.

(4) In all cases, the arbitral tribunal shall decide in accordance with the terms of the contract and shall take into account the usages of the trade applicable to the transaction.

Decision-making by panel of arbitrators

Article 29

In arbitral proceedings with more than one arbitrator, any decision of the arbitral tribunal shall be made, unless otherwise agreed by the parties, by a majority of all its members. However, questions of procedure may be decided by a presiding arbitrator, if so authorised by the parties or all members of the arbitral tribunal.

Settlement

Article 30

(1) If, during arbitral proceedings, the parties settle the dispute, the arbitral tribunal shall terminate the proceedings and, if requested by the parties and not objected to by the arbitral tribunal, record the settlement in the form of an arbitral award on agreed terms.

(2) An award on agreed terms shall be made in accordance with the provisions of Article 31 and shall state that it is an award. Such an award has the same status and effect as any other award on the merits of the case.

Form and contents of award

Article 31

(1) The award shall be made in writing and shall be signed by the arbitrator or arbitrators. In arbitral proceedings with more than one arbitrator, the signatures of the majority of all members of the arbitral tribunal shall suffice, provided that the reason for any omitted signature is stated.

(2) The award shall state the reasons upon which it is based, unless the parties have agreed that no reasons are to be given or the award is an award on agreed terms under Article 30.

(3) The award shall state its date and the place of arbitration as determined in accordance with Article 20(1). The award shall be deemed to have been made at that place.

(4) After the award is made, a copy signed by the arbitrators in accordance with paragraph (1) of this Article shall be delivered to each party.

Termination of proceedings
Article 32

(1) The arbitral proceedings are terminated by the final award or by an order of the arbitral tribunal in accordance with paragraph (2) of this Article.

(2) The arbitral tribunal shall issue an order for the termination of the arbitral proceedings when:

    (a) the claimant withdraws his claim, unless the respondent objects thereto and the arbitral tribunal recognises a legitimate interest on his part in obtaining a final settlement of the dispute;

    (b) the parties agree on the termination of the proceedings;

    (c) the arbitral tribunal finds that the continuation of the proceedings has for any other reason become unnecessary or impossible.

(3) The mandate of the arbitral tribunal terminates with the termination of the arbitral proceedings, subject to the provisions of Articles 33 and 34(4).

Correction and interpretation of award; additional award
Article 33

(1) Within 30 days of receipt of the award, unless another period of time has been agreed upon by the parties:

    (a) a party, with notice to the other party, may request the arbitral tribunal to correct in the award any errors in computation, any clerical or typographical errors or any errors of similar nature;

    (b) if so agreed by the parties, a party, with notice to the other party, may request the arbitral tribunal to give an interpretation of a specific point or part of the award.

If the arbitral tribunal considers the request to be justified, it shall make the correction or give the interpretation within 30 days of receipt of the request. The interpretation shall form part of the award.

(2) The arbitral tribunal may correct any error of the type referred to in paragraph (1)(a) of this Article on its own initiative within 30 days of the date of the award.

(3) Unless otherwise agreed by the parties, a party, with notice to the other party, may request, within 30 days of receipt of the award, the arbitral tribunal to make an additional award as to claims presented in the arbitral proceedings but omitted from the award. If the arbitral tribunal considers the request to be justified, it shall make the additional award within 60 days.

(4) The arbitral tribunal may extend, if necessary, the period of time within which it shall make a correction, interpretation or an additional award under paragraph (1) or (3) of this Article.

(5) The provisions of Article 31 shall apply to a correction or interpretation of the award or to an additional award.

CHAPTER VII – RECOURSE AGAINST AWARD

Application for setting aside as exclusive recourse against arbitral award
Article 34

(1) Recourse to a court against an arbitral award may be made only by an application for setting aside in accordance with paragraphs (2) and (3) of this Article.

(2) An arbitral award may be set aside by the court specified in Article 6 only if:

  (a) the party making the application furnishes proof that:

    (i) a party to the arbitration agreement referred to in Article 7 was under some incapacity; or the said agreement is not valid under the law to which the parties have subjected it or, failing any indication thereon, under the law of this State; or

    (ii) the party making the application was not given proper notice of the appointment of an arbitrator or of the arbitral proceedings or was otherwise unable to present his case; or

    (iii) the award deals with a dispute not contemplated by or not falling within the terms of the submission to arbitration, or contains decisions on matters beyond the scope of the submission to arbitration, provided that, if the decisions on matters submitted to arbitration can be separated from those not so submitted, only that part of the award which contains decisions on matters not submitted to arbitration may be set aside; or

    (iv) the composition of the arbitral tribunal or the arbitral procedure was not in accordance with the agreement of the parties, unless such agreement was in conflict with a provision of this Law from which the parties cannot derogate, or, failing such agreement, was not in accordance with this Law; or

  (b) the court finds that:

    (i) the subject-matter of the dispute is not capable of settlement by arbitration under the law of this State; or

    (ii) the award is in conflict with the public policy of this State.

(3) An application for setting aside may not be made after three months have elapsed from the date on which the party making that application had received the award or, if a request had been made under Article 33, from the date on which that request had been disposed of by the arbitral tribunal.

(4) The court, when asked to set aside an award, may, where appropriate and so requested by a party, suspend the setting aside proceedings for a period of time determined by it in order to give the arbitral tribunal an opportunity to resume the arbitral proceedings or to take such other action as in the arbitral tribunal's opinion will eliminate the grounds for setting aside.

CHAPTER VIII – RECOGNITION AND ENFORCEMENT OF AWARDS

Recognition and enforcement
Article 35

(1) An arbitral award, irrespective of the country in which it was made, shall be recognised as binding and, upon application in writing to the competent court, shall be enforced subject to the provisions of this Article and of Article 36.

(2) The party relying on an award or applying for its enforcement shall supply the duly authenticated original award or a duly certified copy thereof, and the original arbitration agreement referred to in Article 7 or a duly certified copy thereof. If the award or agreement is not made in an official language of this State, the party shall supply a duly certified translation thereof into such language.***

Grounds for refusing recognition or enforcement
Article 36

(1) Recognition or enforcement of an arbitral award, irrespective of the country in which it was made, may be refused only:

(a) at the request of the party against whom it is invoked, if that party furnishes to the competent court where recognition or enforcement is sought proof that:

(i) a party to the arbitration agreement referred to in Article 7 was under some incapacity; or the said agreement is not valid under the law to which the parties have subjected it or, failing any indication thereon, under the law of the country where the award was made; or

(ii) the party against whom the award is invoked was not given proper notice of the appointment of an arbitrator or of the arbitral proceedings or was otherwise unable to present his case; or

---

*** The conditions set forth in this paragraph are intended to set maximum standards. It would, thus, not be contrary to the harmonisation to be achieved by the Model Law if a State retained even less onerous conditions.

(iii)the award deals with a dispute not contemplated by or not falling within the terms of the submission to arbitration, or it contains decisions on matters beyond the scope of the submission to arbitration, provided that, if the decisions on matters submitted to arbitration can be separated from those not so submitted, that part of the award which contains decisions on matters submitted to arbitration may be recognised and enforced; or

(iv)the composition of the arbitral tribunal or the arbitral procedure was not in accordance with the agreement of the parties or, failing such agreement, was not in accordance with the law of the country where the arbitration took place; or

(v) the award has not yet become binding on the parties or has been set aside or suspended by a court of the country in which, or under the law of which, that award was made; or

(b) if the court finds that:

(i) the subject-matter of the dispute is not capable of settlement by arbitration under the law of this State; or

(ii) the recognition or enforcement of the award would be contrary to the public policy of this State.

(2) If an application for setting aside or suspension of an award has been made to a court referred to in paragraph (1)(a)(v) of this Article, the court where recognition or enforcement is sought may, if it considers it proper, adjourn its decision and may also, on the application of the party claiming recognition or enforcement of the award, order the other party to provide appropriate security.

Explanatory Note by the UNCITRAL Secretariat on the Model Law on International Commercial Arbitration*

1. The UNCITRAL Model Law on International Commercial Arbitration was adopted by the United Nations Commission on International Trade Law (UNCITRAL) on 21 June 1985, at the close of the Commission's 18th annual session. The General Assembly, in its resolution 40/72 of 11 December 1985, recommended 'that all States give due consideration to the Model Law on International Commercial Arbitration, in view of the desirability of uniformity of the law of arbitral procedures and the specific needs of international commercial arbitration practice'.

2. The Model Law constitutes a sound and promising basis for the desired harmonisation and improvement of national laws. It covers all stages of the arbitral process from the arbitration agreement to the recognition and enforcement of the arbitral award and reflects a worldwide consensus on the principles and important issues of international arbitration practice. It is acceptable to States of all regions and the different legal or economic systems of the world.

3. The form of a Model Law was chosen as the vehicle for harmonisation and improvement in view of the flexibility it gives to States in preparing new arbitration laws. It is advisable to follow the model as closely as possible since that would be the best contribution to the desired harmonisation and in the best interest of the users of international arbitration, who are primarily foreign parties and their lawyers.

A. BACKGROUND TO THE MODEL LAW

4. The Model Law is designed to meet concerns relating to the current state of national laws on arbitration. The need for improvement and harmonisation is based on findings that domestic laws are often inappropriate for international cases and that considerable disparity exists between them.

---

* This note has been prepared by the Secretariat of the United Nations Commission on International Trade Law (UNCITRAL) for informational purposes only; it is not an official commentary on the Model Law. A commentary prepared by the Secretariat on an earlier draft of the Model Law appears in document A/CN 9/264 (reproduced in UNCITRAL Year-book, vol XVI 1985) (United Nations publication, Sales No E 87 V 4).

1. Inadequacy of domestic laws

5. A global survey of national laws on arbitration revealed considerable disparities not only as regards individual provisions and solutions but also in terms of development and refinement. Some laws may be regarded as outdated, sometimes going back to the 19th century and often equating the arbitral process with court litigation. Other laws may be said to be fragmentary in that they do not address all relevant issues. Even most of those laws which appear to be up-to-date and comprehensive were drafted with domestic arbitration primarily, if not exclusively, in mind. While this approach is understandable in view of the fact that even today the bulk of cases governed by a general arbitration law would be of a purely domestic nature, the unfortunate consequence is that traditional local concepts are imposed on international cases and the needs of modern practice are often not met.

6. The expectations of the parties as expressed in a chosen set of arbitration rules or a 'one-off' arbitration agreement may be frustrated, especially by a mandatory provision of the applicable law. Unexpected and undesired restrictions found in national laws relate, for example, to the parties' ability effectively to submit future disputes to arbitration, to their power to select the arbitrator freely, or to their interest in having the arbitral proceedings conducted according to the agreed rules of procedure and with no more court involvement than is appropriate. Frustrations may also ensue from non-mandatory provisions which may impose undesired requirements on unwary parties who did not provide otherwise. Even the absence of non-mandatory provisions may cause difficulties by not providing answers to the many procedural issues relevant in an arbitration and not always settled in the arbitration agreement.

2. Disparity between national laws

7. Problems and undesired consequences, whether emanating from mandatory or non-mandatory provisions or from a lack of pertinent provisions, are aggravated by the fact that national laws on arbitral procedure differ widely. The differences are a frequent source of concern in international arbitration, where at least one of the parties is, and often both parties are, confronted with foreign and unfamiliar provisions and procedures. For such a party it may be expensive, impractical or impossible to obtain a full and precise account of the law applicable to the arbitration.

8. Uncertainty about the local law with the inherent risk of frustration may adversely affect not only the functioning of the arbitral process

but already the selection of the place of arbitration. A party may well for those reasons hesitate or refuse to agree to a place which otherwise, for practical reasons, would be appropriate in the case at hand. The choice of places of arbitration would thus be widened and the smooth functioning of the arbitral proceedings would be enhanced if States were to adopt the Model Law which is easily recognisable, meets the specific needs of international commercial arbitration and provides an international standard with solutions acceptable to parties from different States and legal systems.

B. SALIENT FEATURES OF THE MODEL LAW

1. Special procedural regime for international commercial arbitration

9. The principles and individual solutions adopted in the Model Law aim at reducing or eliminating the above concerns and difficulties. As a response to the inadequacies and disparities of national laws, the Model Law presents a special legal regime geared to international commercial arbitration, without affecting any relevant treaty in force in the State adopting the Model Law. While the need for uniformity exists only in respect of international cases, the desire of updating and improving the arbitration law may be felt by a State also in respect of non-international cases and could be met by enacting modern legislation based on the Model Law for both categories of cases.

a. Substantive and territorial scope of application

10. The Model Law defines an arbitration as international if 'the parties to an arbitration agreement have, at the time of the conclusion of that agreement, their places of business in different States' (Article 1(3)). The vast majority of situations commonly regarded as international will fall under this criterion. In addition, an arbitration is international if the place of arbitration, the place of contract performance, or the place of the subject-matter of the dispute is situated in a State other than where the parties have their place of business, or if the parties have expressly agreed that the subject-matter of the arbitration agreement relates to more than one country.

11. As regards the term 'commercial', no hard and fast definition could be provided. Article 1 contains a note calling for 'a wide interpretation so as to cover matters arising from all relationships of a commercial nature, whether contractual or not'. The footnote to Article 1 then provides an illustrative list of relationships that are to be considered commercial, thus emphasising the width of the

suggested interpretation and indicating that the determinative test is not based on what the national law may regard as 'commercial'.

12. Another aspect of applicability is what one may call the territorial scope of application. According to Article 1(2), the Model Law as enacted in a given State would apply only if the place of arbitration is in the territory of that State. However, there is an important and reasonable exception. Articles 8(1) and 9 which deal with recognition of arbitration agreements, including their compatibility with interim measures of protection, and Articles 35 and 36 on recognition and enforcement of arbitral awards are given a global scope, ie they apply irrespective of whether the place of arbitration is in that State or in another State and, as regards Articles 8 and 9, even if the place of arbitration is not yet determined.

13. The strict territorial criterion, governing the bulk of the provisions of the Model Law, was adopted for the sake of certainty and in view of the following facts. The place of arbitration is used as the exclusive criterion by the great majority of national laws and, where national laws allow parties to choose the procedural law of a State other than that where the arbitration takes place, experience shows that parties in practice rarely make use of that facility. The Model Law, by its liberal contents, further reduces the need for such choice of a 'foreign' law in lieu of the (Model) Law of the place of arbitration, not the least because it grants parties wide freedom in shaping the rules of the arbitral proceedings. This includes the possibility of incorporating into the arbitration agreement procedural provisions of a 'foreign' law, provided there is no conflict with the few mandatory provisions of the Model Law. Furthermore, the strict territorial criterion is of considerable practical benefit in respect of Articles 11, 13, 14, 16, 27 and 34, which entrust the courts of the respective State with functions of arbitration assistance and supervision.

b. Delimitation of court assistance and supervision

14. As evidenced by recent amendments to arbitration laws, there exists a trend in favour of limiting court involvement in international commercial arbitration. This seems justified in view of the fact that the parties to an arbitration agreement make a conscious decision to exclude court jurisdiction and, in particular in commercial cases, prefer expediency and finality to protracted battles in court.

15. In this spirit, the Model Law envisages court involvement in the following instances. A first group comprises appointment, challenge and termination of the mandate of an arbitrator (Articles

11, 13 and 14), jurisdiction of the arbitral tribunal (Article 16) and setting aside of the arbitral award (Article 34). These instances are listed in Article 6 as functions which should be entrusted, for the sake of centralisation, specialisation and acceleration, to a specially designated court or, as regards Articles 11, 13 and 14, possibly to another authority (eg arbitral institution, chamber of commerce). A second group comprises court assistance in taking evidence (Article 27), recognition of the arbitration agreement, including its compatibility with court ordered interim measures of protection (Articles 8 and 9), and recognition and enforcement of arbitral awards (Articles 35 and 36).

16. Beyond the instances in these two groups, 'no court shall intervene, in matters governed by this Law'. This is stated in the innovative Article 5, which by itself does not take a stand on what is the appropriate role of the courts but guarantees the reader and user that he will find all instances of possible court intervention in this Law, except for matters not regulated by it (eg consolidation of arbitral proceedings, contractual relationship between arbitrators and parties or arbitral institutions, or fixing of costs and fees, including deposits). Especially foreign readers and users, who constitute the majority of potential users and may be viewed as the primary addressees of any special law on international commercial arbitration, will appreciate that they do not have to search outside this Law.

2. Arbitration agreement

17. Chapter II of the Model Law deals with the arbitration agreement, including its recognition by courts. The provisions follow closely Article II of the Convention on the Recognition and Enforcement of Foreign Arbitral Awards (New York, 1958) (hereafter referred to as '1958 New York Convention'), with a number of useful clarifications added.

a. Definition and form of arbitration agreement

18. Article 7(1) recognises the validity and effect of a commitment by the parties to submit to arbitration an existing dispute (*compromis*) or a future dispute (*clause compromissoire*). The latter type of agreement is presently not given full effect under certain national laws.

19. While oral arbitration agreements are found in practice and are recognised by some national laws, Article 7(2) follows the 1958 New York Convention in requiring written form. It widens and

clarifies the definition of written form of Article II(2) of that Convention by adding 'telex or other means of telecommunication which provide a record of the agreement', by covering the submission-type situation of 'an exchange of statements of claim and defence in which the existence of an agreement is alleged by one party and not denied by another', and by providing that 'the reference in a contract to a document' (eg general conditions) 'containing an arbitration clause constitutes an arbitration agreement provided that the contract is in writing and the reference is such as to make that clause part of the contract'.

b. Arbitration agreement and the courts

20. Articles 8 and 9 deal with two important aspects of the complex issue of the relationship between the arbitration agreement and resort to courts. Modelled on Article II(3) of the 1958 New York Convention, Article 8(1) of the Model Law obliges any court to refer the parties to arbitration if seized with a claim on the same subject-matter unless it finds that the arbitration agreement is null and void, inoperative or incapable of being performed. The referral is dependent on a request which a party may make not later than when submitting his first statement on the substance of the dispute. While this provision, where adopted by a State when it adopts the Model Law, by its nature binds merely the courts of that State, it is not restricted to agreements providing for arbitration in that State and, thus, helps to give universal recognition and effect to international commercial arbitration agreements.

21. Article 9 expresses the principle that any interim measures of protection that may be obtained from courts under their procedural law (eg pre-award attachments) are compatible with an arbitration agreement. Like Article 8, this provision is addressed to the courts of a given State, insofar as it determines their granting of interim measures as being compatible with an arbitration agreement, irrespective of the place of arbitration. Insofar as it declares it to be compatible with an arbitration agreement for a party to request such measure from a court, the provision would apply irrespective of whether the request is made to a court of the given State or of any other country. Wherever such request may be made, it may not be relied upon, under the Model Law, as an objection against the existence or effect of an arbitration agreement.

3. Composition of arbitral tribunal

22. Chapter III contains a number of detailed provisions on appointment, challenge, termination of mandate and replacement of an arbitrator. The chapter illustrates the approach of the Model Law in eliminating difficulties arising from inappropriate or fragmentary laws or rules. The approach consists, first, of recognising the freedom of the parties to determine, by reference to an existing set of arbitration rules or by an *ad hoc* agreement, the procedure to be followed, subject to fundamental requirements of fairness and justice. Secondly, where the parties have not used their freedom to lay down the rules of procedure or a particular issue has not been covered, the Model Law ensures, by providing a set of suppletive rules, that the arbitration may commence and proceed effectively to the resolution of the dispute.

23. Where under any procedure, agreed upon by the parties or based upon the suppletive rules of the Model Law, difficulties arise in the process of appointment, challenge or termination of the mandate of an arbitrator, Articles 11, 13 and 14 provide for assistance by courts or other authorities. In view of the urgency of the matter and in order to reduce the risk and effect of any dilatory tactics, instant resort may be had by a party within a short period of time and the decision is not appealable.

4. Jurisdiction of arbitral tribunal

a. *Competence to rule on own jurisdiction*

24. Article 16(1) adopts the two important (not yet generally recognised) principles of 'KompetenzKompetenz' and of separability or autonomy of the arbitration clause. The arbitral tribunal may rule on its own jurisdiction, including any objections with respect to the existence or validity of the arbitration agreement. For that purpose, an arbitration clause shall be treated as an agreement independent of the other terms of the contract, and a decision by the arbitral tribunal that the contract is null and void shall not entail *ipso jure* the invalidity of the arbitration clause. Detailed provisions in paragraph (2) require that any objections relating to the arbitrators' jurisdiction be made at the earliest possible time.

25. The arbitral tribunal's competence to rule on its own jurisdiction, ie on the very foundation of its mandate and power, is, of course, subject to court control. Where the arbitral tribunal rules as a preliminary question that it has jurisdiction, Article 16(3) provides for instant court control in order to avoid unnecessary waste of money and time. However, three procedural safeguards are added

to reduce the risk and effect of dilatory tactics: short time period for resort to court (30 days), court decision is not appealable, and discretion of the arbitral tribunal to continue the proceedings and make an award while the matter is pending with the court. In those less common cases where the arbitral tribunal combines its decision on jurisdiction with an award on the merits, judicial review on the question of jurisdiction is available in setting aside proceedings under Article 34 or in enforcement proceedings under Article 36.

b. *Power to order interim measures*

26. Unlike some national laws, the Model Law empowers the arbitral tribunal, unless otherwise agreed by the parties, to order any party to take an interim measure of protection in respect of the subject-matter of the dispute, if so requested by a party (Article 17). It may be noted that the Article does not deal with enforcement of such measures; any State adopting the Model Law would be free to provide court assistance in this regard.

5. Conduct of arbitral proceedings

27. Chapter V provides the legal framework for a fair and effective conduct of the arbitral proceedings. It opens with two provisions expressing basic principles that permeate the arbitral procedure governed by the Model Law. Article 18 lays down fundamental requirements of procedural justice and Article 19 the rights and powers to determine the rules of procedure.

a. *Fundamental procedural rights of a party*

28. Article 18 embodies the basic principle that the parties shall be treated with equality and each party shall be given a full opportunity of presenting his case. Other provisions implement and specify the basic principle in respect of certain fundamental rights of a party. Article 24(1) provides that, unless the parties have validly agreed that no oral hearings for the presentation of evidence or for oral argument be held, the arbitral tribunal shall hold such hearings at an appropriate stage of the proceedings, if so requested by a party. It should be noted that Article 24(1) deals only with the general right of a party to oral hearings (as an alternative to conducting the proceedings on the basis of documents and other materials) and not with the procedural aspects such as the length, number or timing of hearings.

29. Another fundamental right of a party of being heard and being able to present his case relates to evidence by an expert appointed by the arbitral tribunal. Article 26(2) obliges the expert, after having delivered his written or oral report, to participate in a hearing where the parties may put questions to him and present expert witnesses in order to testify on the points at issue, if such a hearing is requested by a party or deemed necessary by the arbitral tribunal. As another provision aimed at ensuring fairness, objectivity and impartiality, Article 24(3) provides that all statements, documents and other information supplied to the arbitral tribunal by one party shall be communicated to the other party, and that any expert report or evidentiary document on which the arbitral tribunal may rely in making its decision shall be communicated to the parties. In order to enable the parties to be present at any hearing and at any meeting of the arbitral tribunal for inspection purposes, they shall be given sufficient notice in advance (Article 24(2)).

b. *Determination of rules of procedure*

30. Article 19 guarantees the parties' freedom to agree on the procedure to be followed by the arbitral tribunal in conducting the proceedings, subject to a few mandatory provisions on procedure, and empowers the arbitral tribunal, failing agreement by the parties, to conduct the arbitration in such a manner as it considers appropriate. The power conferred upon the arbitral tribunal includes the power to determine the admissibility, relevance, materiality and weight of any evidence.

31. Autonomy of the parties to determine the rules of procedure is of special importance in international cases since it allows the parties to select or tailor the rules according to their specific wishes and needs, unimpeded by traditional domestic concepts and without the earlier mentioned risk of frustration. The supplementary discretion of the arbitral tribunal is equally important in that it allows the tribunal to tailor the conduct of the proceedings to the specific features of the case without restraints of the traditional local law, including any domestic rules on evidence. Moreover, it provides a means for solving any procedural questions not regulated in the arbitration agreement or the Model Law.

32. In addition to the general provisions of Article 19, there are some special provisions using the same approach of granting the parties autonomy and, failing agreement, empowering the arbitral tribunal to decide the matter. Examples of particular practical importance in international cases are Article 20 on the place of arbitration and Article 22 on the language of the proceedings.

c. *Default of a party*

33. Only if due notice was given may the arbitral proceedings be continued in the absence of a party. This applies, in particular, to the failure of a party to appear at a hearing or to produce documentary evidence without showing sufficient cause for the failure (Article 25(c)). The arbitral tribunal may also continue the proceedings where the respondent fails to communicate his statement of defence, while there is no need for continuing the proceedings if the claimant fails to submit his statement of claim (Article 25(a), (b)).

34. Provisions which empower the arbitral tribunal to carry out its task even if one of the parties does not participate are of considerable practical importance since, as experience shows, it is not uncommon that one of the parties has little interest in cooperating and in expediting matters. They would, thus, give international commercial arbitration its necessary effectiveness, within the limits of fundamental requirements of procedural justice.

6. Making of award and termination of proceedings

a. *Rules applicable to substance of dispute*

35. Article 28 deals with the substantive law aspects of arbitration. Under paragraph (1), the arbitral tribunal decides the dispute in accordance with such rules of law as may be agreed by the parties. This provision is significant in two respects. It grants the parties the freedom to choose the applicable substantive law, which is important in view of the fact that a number of national laws do not clearly or fully recognise that right. In addition, by referring to the choice of 'rules of law' instead of 'law', the Model Law gives the parties a wider range of options as regards the designation of the law applicable to the substance of the dispute in that they may, for example, agree on rules of law that have been elaborated by an international forum but have not yet been incorporated into any national legal system. The power of the arbitral tribunal, on the other hand, follows more traditional lines. When the parties have not designated the applicable law, the arbitral tribunal shall apply the law, ie the national law, determined by the conflict of laws rules which it considers applicable.

36. According to Article 28(3), the parties may authorise the arbitral tribunal to decide the dispute *ex aequo et bono* or as *amiable compositeurs*. This type of arbitration is currently not known or used in all legal systems and there exists no uniform understanding as regards the precise scope of the power of the arbitral tribunal. When parties anticipate an uncertainty in this respect, they may

wish to provide a clarification in the arbitration agreement by a more specific authorisation to the arbitral tribunal. Paragraph (4) makes clear that in all cases, ie including an arbitration *ex aequo et bono*, the arbitral tribunal must decide in accordance with the terms of the contract and shall take into account the usages of the trade applicable to the transaction.

b. Making of award and other decisions

37. In its rules on the making of the award (Articles 29–31), the Model Law pays special attention to the rather common case that the arbitral tribunal consists of a plurality of arbitrators (in particular, three). It provides that, in such a case, any award and other decision shall be made by a majority of the arbitrators, except on questions of procedure, which may be left to a presiding arbitrator. The majority principle applies also to the signing of the award, provided that the reason for any omitted signature is stated.

38. Article 31(3) provides that the award shall state the place of arbitration and that it shall be deemed to have been made at that place. As to this presumption, it may be noted that the final making of the award constitutes a legal act, which in practice is not necessarily one factual act but may be done in deliberations at various places, by telephone conversation or correspondence; above all, the award need not be signed by the arbitrators at the same place.

39. The arbitral award must be in writing and state its date. It must also state the reasons on which it is based, unless the parties have agreed otherwise or the award is an award on agreed terms, ie an award which records the terms of an amicable settlement by the parties. It may be added that the Model Law neither requires nor prohibits 'dissenting opinions'.

7. Recourse against award

40. National laws on arbitration, often equating awards with court decisions, provide a variety of means of recourse against arbitral awards, with varying and often long time periods and with extensive lists of grounds that differ widely in the various legal systems. The Model Law attempts to ameliorate this situation, which is of considerable concern to those involved in international commercial arbitration.

a. Application for setting aside as exclusive recourse

41. The first measure of improvement is to allow only one type of recourse, to the exclusion of any other means of recourse regulated

in another procedural law of the State in question. An application for setting aside under Article 34 must be made within three months of receipt of the award. It should be noted that 'recourse' means actively 'attacking' the award; a party is, of course, not precluded from seeking court control by way of defence in enforcement proceedings (Article 36). Furthermore, 'recourse' means resort to a court, ie an organ of the judicial system of a State; a party is not precluded from resorting to an arbitral tribunal of second instance if such a possibility has been agreed upon by the parties (as is common in certain commodity trades).

b. Grounds for setting aside

42. As a further measure of improvement, the Model Law contains an exclusive list of limited grounds on which an award may be set aside. This list is essentially the same as the one in Article 36(1), taken from Article V of the 1958 New York Convention: lack of capacity of parties to conclude arbitration agreement or lack of valid arbitration agreement; lack of notice of appointment of an arbitrator or of the arbitral proceedings or inability of a party to present his case; award deals with matters not covered by submission to arbitration; composition of arbitral tribunal or conduct of arbitral proceedings contrary to effective agreement of parties or, failing agreement, to the Model Law; non-arbitrability of subject-matter of dispute and violation of public policy, which would include serious departures from fundamental notions of procedural justice.

43. Such a parallelism of the grounds for setting aside with those provided in Article V of the 1958 New York Convention for refusal of recognition and enforcement was already adopted in the European Convention on International Commercial Arbitration (Geneva, 1961). Under its Article IX, the decision of a foreign court setting aside an award for a reason other than the ones listed in Article V of the 1958 New York Convention does not constitute a ground for refusing enforcement. The Model Law takes this philosophy one step further by directly limiting the reasons for setting aside.

44. Although the grounds for setting aside are almost identical to those for refusing recognition or enforcement, two practical differences should be noted. Firstly, the grounds relating to public policy, including non-arbitrability, may be different in substance, depending on the State in question (ie State of setting aside or State of enforcement). Secondly, and more importantly, the grounds for refusal of recognition or enforcement are valid and effective only in

the State (or States) where the winning party seeks recognition and enforcement, while the grounds for setting aside have a different impact: the setting aside of an award at the place of origin prevents enforcement of that award in all other countries by virtue of Article V(1)(e) of the 1958 New York Convention and Article 36(1)(a)(v) of the Model Law.

8. Recognition and enforcement of awards

45. The eighth and last chapter of the Model Law deals with recognition and enforcement of awards. Its provisions reflect the significant policy decision that the same rules should apply to arbitral awards whether made in the country of enforcement or abroad, and that those rules should follow closely the 1958 New York Convention.

a. *Towards uniform treatment of all awards irrespective of country of origin*

46. By treating awards rendered in international commercial arbitration in a uniform manner irrespective of where they were made, the Model Law draws a new demarcation line between 'international' and 'non-international' awards instead of the traditional line between 'foreign' and 'domestic' awards. This new line is based on substantive grounds rather than territorial borders, which are inappropriate in view of the limited importance of the place of arbitration in international cases. The place of arbitration is often chosen for reasons of convenience of the parties and the dispute may have little or no connection with the State where the arbitration takes place. Consequently, the recognition and enforcement of 'international' awards, whether 'foreign' or 'domestic', should be governed by the same provisions.

47. By modelling the recognition and enforcement rules on the relevant provisions of the 1958 New York Convention, the Model Law supplements, without conflicting with, the regime of recognition and enforcement created by that successful Convention.

b. *Procedural conditions of recognition and enforcement*

48. Under Article 35(1) any arbitral award, irrespective of the country in which it was made, shall be recognised as binding and enforceable, subject to the provisions of Article 35(2) and of Article 36 (which sets forth the grounds on which recognition or enforcement may be refused). Based on the above consideration of the limited importance of the place of arbitration in international

cases and the desire of overcoming territorial restrictions, reciprocity is not included as a condition for recognition and enforcement.

49. The Model Law does not lay down procedural details of recognition and enforcement since there is no practical need for unifying them, and since they form an intrinsic part of the national procedural law and practice. The Model Law merely sets certain conditions for obtaining enforcement: application in writing, accompanied by the award and the arbitration agreement (Article 35(2)).

c. *Grounds for refusing recognition or enforcement*

50. As noted earlier, the grounds on which recognition or enforcement may be refused under the Model Law are identical to those listed in Article V of the New York Convention. Only, under the Model Law, they are relevant not merely to foreign awards but to all awards rendered in international commercial arbitration. While some provisions of that Convention, in particular as regards their drafting, may have called for improvement, only the first ground on the list (ie 'the parties to the arbitration agreement were, under the law applicable to them, under some incapacity') was modified since it was viewed as containing an incomplete and potentially misleading conflicts rule. Generally, it was deemed desirable to adopt, for the sake of harmony, the same approach and wording as this important Convention.

INDEX

Index

THE AUTHOR

The Author was educated at the Oratory School and then obtained admission to University to read biochemistry and physiology. After leaving school he spent a year and a half in the Pharmaceutical Industry, working as a laboratory technician. This latter employment cured him of the desire to become a biochemist and made him return to his earlier and deeply held wish to become a doctor.

He obtained a place at St Bartholomew's Hospital, London and then joined the merchant navy, serving as a hospital attendant on cruise liners for a year.

Returning to study medicine, he followed a traditional and uneventful course, qualifying in 1975, and then pursued a traditional series of House Officer and Senior House Officer posts.

He entered general practice in 1978, developing interests in medico-legal work, which led him to move into private practice. He developed his medico-legal practice, both personal injury and medical negligence, and by the end of the 1980s had developed a keen interest in alternative means of resolving such disputes. He gained qualifications in both arbitration and mediation and over the years gained considerable practice and experience in both spheres.

He also gained registration in a number of foreign jurisdictions ranging from Eire and Guernsey to South Africa and Hong Kong.

He was appointed to the Bench as a magistrate and became associated with a number of organisations worldwide, including the American Trial Lawyers Association, of which he is a judicial member.

He then founded Dispute Resolution Services Ltd, of which he is Managing Director.